Essential
Student
Algebra

VOLUME TWO

Matrices and Vector Spaces

Withdrawn
University of Waterloo

*Essential
Student
Algebra*

Matrices and Vector Spaces

T. S. BLYTH & E. F. ROBERTSON
University of St Andrews

Withdrawn
University of Waterloo

London   New York
CHAPMAN AND HALL

First published in 1986 by
Chapman and Hall Ltd
11 New Fetter Lane, London EC4P 4EE
Published in the USA by
Chapman and Hall
29 West 35th Street, New York NY 10001

© 1986 T. S. Blyth and E. F. Robertson

Printed in Great Britain by
J. W. Arrowsmith Ltd., Bristol

ISBN 0 412 27870 7

This paperback edition is sold subject to the condition that
it shall not, by way of trade or otherwise, be lent, resold,
hired out, or otherwise circulated without the publisher's
prior consent in any form of binding or cover other than
that in which it is published and without a similar
condition including this condition being imposed on the
subsequent purchaser.

All rights reserved. No part of this book may be reprinted
or reproduced, or utilized in any form or by any electronic,
mechanical or other means, now known or hereafter
invented, including photocopying and recording, or in any
information storage and retrieval system, without
permission in writing from the publisher.

British Library Cataloguing in Publication Data
Blyth, T. S.
Essential student algebra.
Vol 2: Matrices and vector spaces
1. Algebra
I. Title   II. Robertson, E. F.
512   QA155

ISBN 0-412-27870-7

Contents

Withdrawn
University of Waterloo

Preface

If, as it is often said, mathematics is the queen of science then algebra is surely the jewel in her crown. In the course of its vast development over the last half-century, algebra has emerged as the subject in which one can observe pure mathematical reasoning at its best. Its elegance is matched only by the ever-increasing number of its applications to an extraordinarily wide range of topics in areas other than 'pure' mathematics.

Here our objective is to present, in the form of a series of five concise volumes, the fundamentals of the subject. Broadly speaking, we have covered in all the now traditional syllabus that is found in first and second year university courses, as well as some third year material. Further study would be at the level of 'honours options'. The reasoning that lies behind this modular presentation is simple, namely to allow the student (be he a mathematician or not) to read the subject in a way that is more appropriate to the length, content, and extent, of the various courses he has to take.

Although we have taken great pains to include a wide selection of illustrative examples, we have not included any exercises. For a suitable companion collection of worked examples, we would refer the reader to our series *Algebra through practice* (Cambridge University Press), the first five books of which are appropriate to the material covered here.

T.S.B., E.F.R.

CHAPTER ONE

The algebra of matrices

If m and n are positive integers then by a *matrix of size m by n* (or an *$m \times n$ matrix*) we shall mean a rectangular array consisting of mn numbers displayed in m rows and n columns :

$$\begin{bmatrix} x_{11} & x_{12} & x_{13} & \cdots & x_{1n} \\ x_{21} & x_{22} & x_{23} & \cdots & x_{2n} \\ x_{31} & x_{32} & x_{33} & \cdots & x_{3n} \\ \vdots & \vdots & \vdots & & \vdots \\ x_{m1} & x_{m2} & x_{m3} & \cdots & x_{mn} \end{bmatrix}$$

Note that the indexing is such that the first suffix gives the number of the *row* and the second suffix is that of the *column*, so that the entry x_{pq} appears at the intersection of the p-th row and the q-th column.

We shall often find it convenient to abbreviate the above display to simply $[x_{ij}]_{m \times n}$ and refer to x_{ij} as the *(i, j)-th element* of the matrix. The expression $X = [x_{ij}]_{m \times n}$ will be taken to mean 'X is the $m \times n$ matrix whose (i, j)-th element is x_{ij}'.

Example The matrix

$$X = \begin{bmatrix} 1 & 1 & 1 \\ 2 & 2^2 & 2^3 \\ 3 & 3^2 & 3^3 \end{bmatrix}$$

can be expressed as $X = [x_{ij}]_{3 \times 3}$ where $x_{ij} = i^j$.

Example The matrix

$$X = \begin{bmatrix} a & a & a \\ 0 & a & a \\ 0 & 0 & a \end{bmatrix}$$

can be expressed as $X = [x_{ij}]_{3 \times 3}$ where

$$x_{ij} = \begin{cases} a & \text{if } i \leq j; \\ 0 & \text{otherwise.} \end{cases}$$

Example The matrix

$$X = \begin{bmatrix} 1 & 0 & 0 & \dots & 0 \\ e & 1 & 0 & \dots & 0 \\ e^2 & e & 1 & \dots & 0 \\ e^3 & e^2 & e & \dots & 0 \\ \vdots & \vdots & \vdots & & \vdots \\ e^{n-1} & e^{n-2} & e^{n-3} & \dots & 1 \end{bmatrix}$$

can be expressed as $X = [x_{ij}]_{n \times n}$ where

$$x_{ij} = \begin{cases} e^{i-j} & \text{if } i \geq j; \\ 0 & \text{otherwise.} \end{cases}$$

Before we can develop an algebra for matrices, it is essential that we know what is meant by saying that two matrices are *equal*. Common sense dictates that this should happen only if the matrices in question are of the same size and have corresponding entries (numbers) equal.

Definition If $A = [a_{ij}]_{m \times n}$ and $B = [b_{ij}]_{p \times q}$ then we say that A and B are *equal* (and write $A = B$) if, and only if,

(1) $m = p$ and $n = q$;
(2) $a_{ij} = b_{ij}$ for all i, j.

The algebraic system that we shall develop for matrices will have many of the familiar properties enjoyed by the system of real numbers. However, as we shall see, there are some very striking differences.

Definition Given $m \times n$ matrices $A = [a_{ij}]$ and $B = [b_{ij}]$, we define the *sum* $A + B$ to be the $m \times n$ matrix whose (i, j)-th element is $a_{ij} + b_{ij}$.

Note that the sum $A + B$ is defined only when A and B are each of size $m \times n$; and to obtain the sum we simply add corresponding elements. Note also that $A + B$ is thus also of size $m \times n$.

1.1 Theorem *Addition of matrices is*

(1) *commutative* [*in the sense that if A, B are of the same size then $A + B = B + A$*];

(2) *associative* [*in the sense that if A, B, C are of the same size then $A + (B + C) = (A + B) + C$*].

Proof (1) If $A = [a_{ij}]_{m \times n}$ and $B = [b_{ij}]_{m \times n}$ then by the above definition $A + B = [a_{ij} + b_{ij}]_{m \times n}$ and $B + A = [b_{ij} + a_{ij}]_{m \times n}$. But ordinary addition of numbers is commutative, so $a_{ij} + b_{ij} = b_{ij} + a_{ij}$ for all i, j and hence, by the definition of equality for matrices, we have $A + B = B + A$.

(2) If $A = [a_{ij}]_{m \times n}, B = [b_{ij}]_{m \times n}$ and $C = [c_{ij}]_{m \times n}$ then the (i, j)-th element of $A + (B + C)$ is $a_{ij} + (b_{ij} + c_{ij})$, and that of $(A + B) + C$ is $(a_{ij} + b_{ij}) + c_{ij}$. Since ordinary addition of numbers is associative, we have $a_{ij} + (b_{ij} + c_{ij}) = (a_{ij} + b_{ij}) + c_{ij}$ for all i, j and hence, by the definition of equality for matrices, $A + (B + C) = (A + B) + C$. $\diamond$

Because of 1.1(2), we shall agree to write $A + B + C$ for either $A + (B + C)$ or $(A + B) + C$.

1.2 Theorem *There is a unique $m \times n$ matrix M such that $A + M = A$ for every $m \times n$ matrix A.*

Proof Consider the $m \times n$ matrix $M = [m_{ij}]$ in which every $m_{ij} = 0$. For every $m \times n$ matrix A we have $A + M = [a_{ij} + m_{ij}] = [a_{ij} + 0] = [a_{ij}] = A$. To establish the uniqueness of this matrix M, suppose that $B = [b_{ij}]$ is an $m \times n$ matrix such that $A + B = A$ for every $m \times n$ matrix A. Then in particular $M + B = M$. But, taking B instead of A in the property for M, we have $B + M = B$. It now follows by 1.1(1) that $B = M$. $\diamond$

$\left\{ \begin{array}{l} M + B = B + M \\ M = B \end{array} \right.$

Definition The unique matrix M described in 1.2 is called the *$m \times n$ zero matrix* and will be denoted by $0_{m \times n}$, or simply 0 if no confusion arises. Thus $0_{m \times n}$ is the $m \times n$ matrix all of whose entries are 0.

1.3 Theorem *For every $m \times n$ matrix A there is a unique $m \times n$ matrix B such that $A + B = 0$.*

Proof Given $A = [a_{ij}]_{m \times n}$, let $B = [-a_{ij}]_{m \times n}$. Then clearly $A + B = [a_{ij} + (-a_{ij})] = 0$. To establish the uniqueness of such a matrix B, suppose that $C = [c_{ij}]$ is also an $m \times n$ matrix such that $A + C = 0$. Then for all i, j we have $a_{ij} + c_{ij} = 0$ and consequently $c_{ij} = -a_{ij}$, which means that $C = B$. $\diamond$

Definition The unique matrix B described in 1.3 is called the *additive inverse* of A and will be denoted by $-A$. Thus $-A$ is the matrix whose elements are the additive inverses of the corresponding elements of A.

Given real numbers x, y the difference $x - y$ is defined to be $x + (-y)$. For matrices A, B of the same size we shall write $A - B$ for $A + (-B)$, the operation '$-$' so defined being called *subtraction* of matrices.

So far, our matrix algebra has been confined to the operation of addition, which is a simple extension of the same notion for numbers. We shall now consider how the notion of multiplication for numbers can be extended to matrices. This, however, is not so straightforward. There are in fact two basic multiplications that can be defined; the first 'multiplies' a matrix by a number, and the second 'multiplies' a matrix by another matrix.

Definition Given a matrix A and a number λ, we define the *product of A by λ* to be the matrix, denoted by λA, that is obtained from A by multiplying every element of A by λ. Thus, if $A = [a_{ij}]_{m \times n}$ then $\lambda A = [\lambda a_{ij}]_{m \times n}$.

This operation is traditionally called *multiplying a matrix by a scalar* (where the word *scalar* is taken to be synonymous with *number*). The principal properties of this operation are listed in the following result.

1.4 Theorem *If A, B are $m \times n$ matrices then, for all scalars λ and μ,*

(1) $\lambda(A + B) = \lambda A + \lambda B$;
(2) $(\lambda + \mu)A = \lambda A + \mu A$;
(3) $\lambda(\mu A) = (\lambda \mu)A$;
(4) $(-1)A = -A$;
(5) $0A = 0_{m \times n}$.

Proof Let $A = [a_{ij}]_{m \times n}$ and $B = [b_{ij}]_{m \times n}$. Then we have

(1) $\lambda(A + B) = [\lambda(a_{ij} + b_{ij})] = [\lambda a_{ij} + \lambda b_{ij}] = [\lambda a_{ij}] + [\lambda b_{ij}] = \lambda A + \lambda B;$

(2) $(\lambda + \mu)A = [(\lambda + \mu)a_{ij}] = [\lambda a_{ij} + \mu a_{ij}] = [\lambda a_{ij}] + [\mu a_{ij}] = \lambda A + \mu A;$

(3) $\lambda(\mu A) = \lambda[\mu a_{ij}] = [\lambda \mu a_{ij}] = (\lambda \mu)A;$

(4) $(-1)A = [(-1)a_{ij}] = [-a_{ij}] = -A;$

(5) $0A = [0a_{ij}] = [0] = 0_{m \times n}.$ ◇

Note that for every positive integer n we have

$$nA = A + A + \cdots + A \quad (n \text{ terms}).$$

This follows immediately from the definition of λA; for the (i, j)-th element of nA is $na_{ij} = a_{ij} + \cdots + a_{ij}$, there being n terms in the summation.

Example Given the matrices

$$I = \begin{bmatrix} 1 & 0 & 0 \\ 0 & 1 & 0 \\ 0 & 0 & 1 \end{bmatrix}, \qquad J = \begin{bmatrix} 1 & 1 & 1 \\ 1 & 1 & 1 \\ 1 & 1 & 1 \end{bmatrix}$$

the matrix X such that $X + I = 2(X - J)$ is determined by using the algebra. We have $X + I = 2X - 2J$ and so

$$X = I + 2J = \begin{bmatrix} 1 & 0 & 0 \\ 0 & 1 & 0 \\ 0 & 0 & 1 \end{bmatrix} + \begin{bmatrix} 2 & 2 & 2 \\ 2 & 2 & 2 \\ 2 & 2 & 2 \end{bmatrix} = \begin{bmatrix} 3 & 2 & 2 \\ 2 & 3 & 2 \\ 2 & 2 & 3 \end{bmatrix}.$$

We shall now describe the operation that is called *matrix multiplication*. This is the 'multiplication' of one matrix by another. At first sight this concept (due to Cayley) appears to be a most curious one. Whilst it has in fact a very natural interpretation in an algebraic context that we shall see later, we shall for the present simply accept it without asking how it arises; however, its importance, particularly in the applications of matrix algebra, will be illustrated in the next chapter.

Definition Let $A = [a_{ij}]_{m \times n}$ and $B = [b_{ij}]_{n \times p}$. Then we define the *product* AB to be the $m \times p$ matrix whose (i, j)-th element is

$$[AB]_{ij} = \sum_{k=1}^{n} a_{ik}b_{kj} = a_{i1}b_{1j} + a_{i2}b_{2j} + a_{i3}b_{3j} + \cdots + a_{in}b_{nj}.$$

To see exactly what the above formula means, let us fix i and j, say $i = 1$ and $j = 2$. The $(1, 2)$-th element of AB is then

$$\sum_{k=1}^{n} a_{1k}b_{k2} = a_{11}b_{12} + a_{12}b_{22} + a_{13}b_{32} + \cdots + a_{1n}b_{n2}.$$

Thus, to obtain the $(1, 2)$-th element of AB we multiply the elements of the first *row* of A by the corresponding elements in the second *column* of B and sum the products so formed :

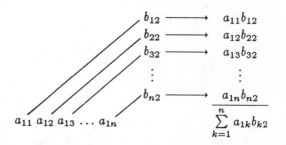

More generally, to determine the (p, q)-th element of AB we multiply the elements of the p-th *row* of A by the corresponding elements in the q-th *column* of B and sum the products so formed. It is important to note that there are no elements 'left over' in the sense that this sum of products is always defined, for in the definition of the matrix product AB the number n of columns of A is the same as the number of rows of B.

Example Consider the matrices

$$A = \begin{bmatrix} 0 & 1 & 0 \\ 2 & 3 & 1 \end{bmatrix}, \qquad B = \begin{bmatrix} 2 & 0 \\ 1 & 2 \\ 1 & 1 \end{bmatrix}.$$

The product AB is defined since A is of size 2×3 and B is of size 3×2; moreover, AB is of size 2×2. We have

$$AB = \begin{bmatrix} 0 \cdot 2 + 1 \cdot 1 + 0 \cdot 1 & 0 \cdot 0 + 1 \cdot 2 + 0 \cdot 1 \\ 2 \cdot 2 + 3 \cdot 1 + 1 \cdot 1 & 2 \cdot 0 + 3 \cdot 2 + 1 \cdot 1 \end{bmatrix} = \begin{bmatrix} 1 & 2 \\ 8 & 7 \end{bmatrix}.$$

Note that in this case the product BA is also defined (since B has the same number of columns as A has rows). The product BA is of size 3×3 :

$$BA = \begin{bmatrix} 2 \cdot 0 + 0 \cdot 2 & 2 \cdot 1 + 0 \cdot 3 & 2 \cdot 0 + 0 \cdot 1 \\ 1 \cdot 0 + 2 \cdot 2 & 1 \cdot 1 + 2 \cdot 3 & 1 \cdot 0 + 2 \cdot 1 \\ 1 \cdot 0 + 1 \cdot 2 & 1 \cdot 1 + 1 \cdot 3 & 1 \cdot 0 + 1 \cdot 1 \end{bmatrix} = \begin{bmatrix} 0 & 2 & 0 \\ 4 & 7 & 2 \\ 2 & 4 & 1 \end{bmatrix}.$$

The above example exhibits a curious fact about matrix multiplication, namely that if AB and BA are defined then these products need not be equal. Indeed, as we have just seen, AB and BA need not be of the same size. It is also possible for AB and BA to be defined and of the same size and still be unequal :

Example Consider the matrices

$$A = \begin{bmatrix} 0 & 1 \\ 0 & 0 \end{bmatrix}, \quad B = \begin{bmatrix} 1 & 0 \\ 0 & 0 \end{bmatrix}.$$

Here we have $AB = 0$ and $BA = A$.

We now consider the basic properties of matrix multiplication.

1.5 Theorem *Matrix multiplication is*

(1) *non-commutative [in the sense that, when the products are defined, $AB \neq BA$ in general];*

(2) *associative [in the sense that, when the products are defined, $A(BC) = (AB)C$].*

Proof (1) This has been observed in the above example.

(2) For $A(BC)$ to be defined we require the respective sizes to be $m \times n, n \times p, p \times q$, in which case the product $(AB)C$ is also defined, and conversely. Computing the (i,j)-th element of $A(BC)$, we obtain

$$[A(BC)]_{ij} = \sum_{k=1}^{n} a_{ik}[BC]_{kj} = \sum_{k=1}^{n} a_{ik} \left(\sum_{t=1}^{p} b_{kt}c_{tj} \right)$$

$$= \sum_{k=1}^{n} \sum_{t=1}^{p} a_{ik}b_{kt}c_{tj}.$$

If we now compute the (i,j)-th element of $(AB)C$, we obtain the same :

$$[(AB)C]_{ij} = \sum_{t=1}^{p} [AB]_{it} c_{tj} = \sum_{t=1}^{p} \left(\sum_{k=1}^{n} a_{ik} b_{kt} \right) c_{tj}$$
$$= \sum_{t=1}^{p} \sum_{k=1}^{n} a_{ik} b_{kt} c_{tj}.$$

Consequently we see that $A(BC) = (AB)C$. $\diamond$

Because of 1.5(2) we shall write ABC for either $A(BC)$ or $(AB)C$. Also, for every positive integer n, we shall write A^n for $AA \cdots A$ (n terms).

Matrix multiplication and matrix addition are connected by the following *distributive laws*.

1.6 Theorem *When the relevant sums and products are defined, we have*

$$A(B+C) = AB + AC \qquad and \qquad (B+C)A = BA + CA.$$

Proof We require A to be of size $m \times n$ and B, C to be of size $n \times p$, in which case

$$[A(B+C)]_{ij} = \sum_{k=1}^{n} a_{ik}[B+C]_{kj} = \sum_{k=1}^{n} a_{ik}(b_{kj} + c_{kj})$$
$$= \sum_{k=1}^{n} a_{ik} b_{kj} + \sum_{k=1}^{n} a_{ik} c_{kj}$$
$$= [AB]_{ij} + [AC]_{ij}$$
$$= [AB + AC]_{ij}$$

and it follows that $A(B+C) = AB + AC$. The other distributive law is established similarly. $\diamond$

Matrix multiplication is also connected with multiplication by scalars.

1.7 Theorem *If AB is defined then for all scalars λ we have*

$$\lambda(AB) = (\lambda A)B = A(\lambda B).$$

Proof It suffices to compute the (i,j)-th elements of the three mixed products. We have in fact

$$\lambda \left(\sum_{k=1}^{n} a_{ik} b_{kj} \right) = \sum_{k=1}^{n} (\lambda a_{ik}) b_{kj} = \sum_{k=1}^{n} a_{ik}(\lambda b_{kj}),$$

from which the result follows. $\diamond$

Definition A matrix is said to be *square* if it is of size $n \times n$.

Our next result is the multiplicative analogue of 1.2, but the reader should note carefully that it applies only in the case of square matrices.

1.8 Theorem *There is a unique $n \times n$ matrix M such that $AM = A = MA$ for every $n \times n$ matrix A.*

Proof Consider the $n \times n$ matrix

$$M = \begin{bmatrix} 1 & 0 & 0 & \ldots & 0 \\ 0 & 1 & 0 & \ldots & 0 \\ 0 & 0 & 1 & \ldots & 0 \\ \vdots & \vdots & \vdots & & \vdots \\ 0 & 0 & 0 & \ldots & 1 \end{bmatrix}.$$

More precisely, if we define the *Kronecker symbol* δ_{ij} by

$$\delta_{ij} = \begin{cases} 1 & \text{if } i = j; \\ 0 & \text{otherwise,} \end{cases}$$

then we have $M = [\delta_{ij}]_{n \times n}$. If $A = [a_{ij}]_{n \times n}$ then, computing the (i, j)-th element of AM, we obtain

$$[AM]_{ij} = \sum_{k=1}^{n} a_{ik} \delta_{kj} = a_{ij},$$

the last equality following from the fact that every term in the summation is 0 except that in which $k = j$, and this term is $a_{ij}1 = a_{ij}$. We deduce, therefore, that $AM = A$. Similarly, we have $MA = A$. This then establishes the existence of such a matrix M. To obtain its uniqueness, suppose that P is also an $n \times n$ matrix such that $AP = A = PA$ for every $n \times n$ matrix A. Then in particular we have $MP = M = PM$. But, by the same property for M, we have $MP = P = PM$. Thus we see that $P = M$. $\diamond$

Definition The unique matrix M described in 1.8 is called the $n \times n$ *identity matrix* and will be denoted by I_n.

Note that I_n has all its 'diagonal' entries equal to 1 and all other entries 0. This is a special case of the following important type of square matrix.

Definition A square matrix $D = [d_{ij}]_{n \times n}$ is said to be *diagonal* if $d_{ij} = 0$ whenever $i \neq j$. Less formally, D is diagonal when all the entries off the main diagonal are 0.

It should be noted carefully that there is no multiplicative analogue of 1.3; for example, if

$$A = \begin{bmatrix} 0 & 1 \\ 0 & 0 \end{bmatrix}$$

then we have

$$\begin{bmatrix} a & b \\ c & d \end{bmatrix} \begin{bmatrix} 0 & 1 \\ 0 & 0 \end{bmatrix} = \begin{bmatrix} 0 & a \\ 0 & c \end{bmatrix},$$

so there is no matrix M such that $MA = I_2$.

There are several other curious properties of matrix multiplication. We mention in particular the following examples, which illustrate in a very simple way the fact that matrix multiplication has to be treated with some care since many of the familiar laws of high-school algebra break down in this new algebraic system.

Example If A, B are $n \times n$ matrices then by 1.6 we have

$$(A + B)^2 = (A + B)(A + B) = A(A + B) + B(A + B)$$
$$= A^2 + AB + BA + B^2.$$

It follows that the equality $(A + B)^2 = A^2 + 2AB + B^2$ holds if and only if $AB = BA$.

Definition If A, B are $n \times n$ matrices then A, B are said to *commute* if $AB = BA$.

Example If A and B commute then a simple inductive argument shows that the usual binomial expansion is valid for $(A + B)^n$. The converse is not true in general. In fact, the reader may care to verify that if

$$A = \begin{bmatrix} 0 & 1 \\ 0 & 1 \end{bmatrix} \quad \text{and} \quad B = \begin{bmatrix} -1 & -1 \\ 0 & 0 \end{bmatrix}$$

then $(A + B)^3 = A^3 + 3A^2B + 3AB^2 + B^3$ but $AB \neq BA$.

Example If we say that a matrix M is a *square root* of the matrix A whenever $M^2 = A$ then the simple equation

$$\begin{bmatrix} 0 & \lambda \\ \lambda^{-1} & 0 \end{bmatrix} \begin{bmatrix} 0 & \lambda \\ \lambda^{-1} & 0 \end{bmatrix} = I_2$$

shows that I_2 has infinitely many square roots!

Definition If A is an $m \times n$ matrix then by the *transpose* of A we shall mean the $n \times m$ matrix whose (i,j)-th element is the (j,i)-th element of A. More precisely, if $A = [a_{ij}]_{m \times n}$ then the transpose of A is the $n \times m$ matrix, denoted by A^t, such that $[A^t]_{ij} = a_{ji}$. (Note the reversal of indices.)

The principal properties of transposition are listed in the following result.

1.9 Theorem *When the relevant sums and products are defined, we have*

$$(A^t)^t = A, \quad (A+B)^t = A^t + B^t, \quad (\lambda A)^t = \lambda A^t, \quad (AB)^t = B^t A^t.$$

Proof The first three equalities are immediate from the definition. To prove that $(AB)^t = B^t A^t$ (note the reversal), suppose that $A = [a_{ij}]_{m \times n}$ and $B = [b_{ij}]_{n \times p}$. Then $(AB)^t$ and $B^t A^t$ are each of size $p \times m$. Since

$$[B^t A^t]_{ij} = \sum_{k=1}^{n} [B^t]_{ik} [A^t]_{kj} = \sum_{k=1}^{n} b_{ki} a_{jk} = \sum_{k=1}^{n} a_{jk} b_{ki} = [AB]_{ji},$$

we deduce that $B^t A^t = (AB)^t$. $\Diamond$

Definition A square matrix A is said to be *symmetric* if $A^t = A$; and *skew-symmetric* if $A^t = -A$.

Example For every square matrix A the matrix $A + A^t$ is symmetric and the matrix $A - A^t$ is skew-symmetric. In fact, by 1.9, we have $(A + A^t)^t = A^t + (A^t)^t = A^t + A$ so $A + A^t$ is symmetric, and $(A - A^t)^t = A^t - (A^t)^t = A^t - A = -(A - A^t)$ so $A - A^t$ is skew-symmetric.

Example Every square matrix can be expressed in a unique way as the sum of a symmetric matrix and a skew-symmetric matrix. Indeed, the equality

$$A = \tfrac{1}{2}(A + A^t) + \tfrac{1}{2}(A - A^t)$$

shows that such an expression is possible. As for the uniqueness, suppose that $A = B + C$ where B is symmetric and C is skew-symmetric. Then $A^t = B^t + C^t = B - C$ and it follows from these equations that $B = \tfrac{1}{2}(A + A^t)$ and $C = \tfrac{1}{2}(A - A^t)$.

CHAPTER TWO

Some applications
of matrices

We shall now give brief descriptions of some situations to
which matrix theory finds a natural application, and some problems to which the solutions are determined by the algebra we
have developed. Some of these applications will be dealt with
in greater detail later.

1 Analytic geometry

In analytic geometry, various transformations of the coordinate axes may be described using matrices. For example, in
the two-dimensional cartesian plane suppose that we rotate the
coordinate axes in an anti-clockwise direction through an angle
ϑ, as illustrated in the diagram

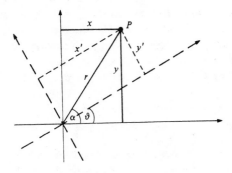

Let us compute the 'new' coordinates (x', y') of the point P
whose 'old' coordinates are (x, y). Referring to the diagram, we

have $x = r \cos \alpha$ and $y = r \sin \alpha$ and so

$$
\begin{aligned}
x' = r \cos(\alpha - \vartheta) &= r \cos \alpha \cos \vartheta + r \sin \alpha \sin \vartheta \\
&= x \cos \vartheta + y \sin \vartheta; \\
y' = r \sin(\alpha - \vartheta) &= r \sin \alpha \cos \vartheta - r \cos \alpha \sin \vartheta \\
&= y \cos \vartheta - x \sin \vartheta.
\end{aligned}
$$

These equations give x', y' in terms of x, y and can be expressed in the matrix form

$$
\begin{bmatrix} x' \\ y' \end{bmatrix} = \begin{bmatrix} \cos \vartheta & \sin \vartheta \\ -\sin \vartheta & \cos \vartheta \end{bmatrix} \begin{bmatrix} x \\ y \end{bmatrix}.
$$

The 2×2 matrix

$$
R_\vartheta = \begin{bmatrix} \cos \vartheta & \sin \vartheta \\ -\sin \vartheta & \cos \vartheta \end{bmatrix}
$$

is called the *rotation matrix* associated with ϑ. A simple calculation reveals that $R_\vartheta R_\vartheta^t = I_2 = R_\vartheta^t R_\vartheta$.

Definition An $n \times n$ matrix A is said to be *orthogonal* if

$$
AA^t = I_n = A^t A.
$$

Thus, to every rotation of axes in two dimensions there is associated a real orthogonal matrix ('real' in the sense that its elements are real numbers). Consider now the effect of one rotation followed by another. Suppose that we transform (x, y) into (x', y') by a rotation through ϑ, then (x', y') into (x'', y'') by a rotation through φ. Then we have

$$
\begin{aligned}
\begin{bmatrix} x'' \\ y'' \end{bmatrix} &= \begin{bmatrix} \cos \varphi & \sin \varphi \\ -\sin \varphi & \cos \varphi \end{bmatrix} \begin{bmatrix} x' \\ y' \end{bmatrix} \\
&= \begin{bmatrix} \cos \varphi & \sin \varphi \\ -\sin \varphi & \cos \varphi \end{bmatrix} \begin{bmatrix} \cos \vartheta & \sin \vartheta \\ -\sin \vartheta & \cos \vartheta \end{bmatrix} \begin{bmatrix} x \\ y \end{bmatrix}.
\end{aligned}
$$

This suggests that the effect of one rotation followed by another can be described by the product of the rotation matrices in question. Now it is intuitively clear that the order in which we perform the rotations does not matter, the final frame of reference being the same whether we first rotate through ϑ then through φ or whether we rotate first through φ then through ϑ. Intuitively, therefore, we can assert that *rotation matrices commute*. That this is indeed the case follows from the identities

$$R_\vartheta R_\varphi = R_{\vartheta+\varphi} = R_\varphi R_\vartheta$$

which the reader can readily verify using standard trigonometric identities for $\cos(\vartheta + \varphi)$ and $\sin(\vartheta + \varphi)$.

2 Systems of linear equations

We have seen above how a certain pair of equations can be expressed using matrix products. Let us now consider the general case. By a *system of m linear equations in the n unknowns* $x_1, \ldots, x_n$ we shall mean a list of equations of the form

$$a_{11}x_1 + a_{12}x_2 + a_{13}x_3 + \cdots + a_{1n}x_n = b_1$$
$$a_{21}x_1 + a_{22}x_2 + a_{23}x_3 + \cdots + a_{2n}x_n = b_2$$
$$a_{31}x_1 + a_{32}x_2 + a_{33}x_3 + \cdots + a_{3n}x_n = b_3$$
$$\vdots$$
$$a_{m1}x_1 + a_{m2}x_2 + a_{m3}x_3 + \cdots + a_{mn}x_n = b_m$$

where the a_{ij} and b_i are numbers. This system can be expressed succinctly as a single matrix equation

$$A\mathbf{x} = \mathbf{b}$$

where $A = [a_{ij}]_{m \times n}$ and $\mathbf{x}, \mathbf{b}$ are the *column matrices* given by

$$\mathbf{x} = \begin{bmatrix} x_1 \\ x_2 \\ \vdots \\ x_n \end{bmatrix}, \quad \mathbf{b} = \begin{bmatrix} b_1 \\ b_2 \\ \vdots \\ b_m \end{bmatrix}.$$

The $m \times n$ matrix A is called the *coefficient matrix* of the system. Note that it transforms a column matrix of length n into a column matrix of length m. In the case where $\mathbf{b} = \mathbf{0}$ (i.e.

every $b_i = 0$) we say that the system is *homogeneous*. Adjoining to A the column **b**, we obtain an $m \times (n + 1)$ matrix which we write as $A|\mathbf{b}$ and call the *augmented matrix* of the system. Whether or not a given system of linear equations has a solution depends heavily on the augmented matrix of the system. How to determine all the solutions (when they exist) will be the object of study in the next chapter.

3 Equilibrium-seeking systems

Consider the following situation. In a population study, a certain proportion of city dwellers move into the country every year and a certain proportion of country dwellers decide to become city dwellers. A similar situation occurs in national employment where a certain percentage of unemployed people find jobs and a certain percentage of employed people become unemployed. Mathematically, these situations are essentially the same. The problem that poses itself is how to describe this situation in a concrete mathematical way, and in so doing determine whether such a system reaches a 'steady state'. Our objective now is to show how matrices can be used to solve this problem.

To be more specific, let us suppose that 75% of the unemployed at the beginning of a year find jobs during the year, and that 5% of people with jobs become unemployed during the year. These proportions are somewhat optimistic, and might lead one to conjecture that 'sooner or later' everyone will have a job. But these figures are chosen to illustrate the point we wish to make, namely that the system 'settles down' to fixed proportions. The situation can be described compactly by the following matrix and its obvious interpretation :

	unemployed	employed
into unemployment	$\frac{1}{4}$	$\frac{1}{20}$
into employment	$\frac{3}{4}$	$\frac{19}{20}$

Suppose now that the fraction of the population that is originally unemployed is L_0 and that the fraction of the population that is originally employed is $M_0 = 1 - L_0$. We represent this state of affairs by the matrix

$$\begin{bmatrix} L_0 \\ M_0 \end{bmatrix}.$$

In a more general way, we let the matrix

$$\begin{bmatrix} L_i \\ M_i \end{bmatrix}$$

signify the proportions of the unemployed/employed population at the end of the i-th year. At the end of the first year we have

$$L_1 = \tfrac{1}{4}L_0 + \tfrac{1}{20}M_0$$
$$M_1 = \tfrac{3}{4}L_0 + \tfrac{19}{20}M_0$$

and we can express these equations in the matrix form

$$\begin{bmatrix} L_1 \\ M_1 \end{bmatrix} = \begin{bmatrix} \tfrac{1}{4} & \tfrac{1}{20} \\ \tfrac{3}{4} & \tfrac{19}{20} \end{bmatrix} \begin{bmatrix} L_0 \\ M_0 \end{bmatrix}$$

which involves the 2×2 matrix introduced above. Similarly, at the end of the second year we have

$$L_2 = \tfrac{1}{4}L_1 + \tfrac{1}{20}M_1$$
$$M_2 = \tfrac{3}{4}L_1 + \tfrac{19}{20}M_1$$

and consequently

$$\begin{bmatrix} L_2 \\ M_2 \end{bmatrix} = \begin{bmatrix} \tfrac{1}{4} & \tfrac{1}{20} \\ \tfrac{3}{4} & \tfrac{19}{20} \end{bmatrix} \begin{bmatrix} L_1 \\ M_1 \end{bmatrix} = \begin{bmatrix} \tfrac{1}{4} & \tfrac{1}{20} \\ \tfrac{3}{4} & \tfrac{19}{20} \end{bmatrix}^2 \begin{bmatrix} L_0 \\ M_0 \end{bmatrix}.$$

Using induction, we can thus say that at the end of the k-th year the relationship between L_k, M_k and L_0, M_0 is given by

$$\begin{bmatrix} L_k \\ M_k \end{bmatrix} = \begin{bmatrix} \tfrac{1}{4} & \tfrac{1}{20} \\ \tfrac{3}{4} & \tfrac{19}{20} \end{bmatrix}^k \begin{bmatrix} L_0 \\ M_0 \end{bmatrix}.$$

Now it can be shown that, for all positive integers k,

$$\begin{bmatrix} \tfrac{1}{4} & \tfrac{1}{20} \\ \tfrac{3}{4} & \tfrac{19}{20} \end{bmatrix}^k = \tfrac{1}{16} \begin{bmatrix} 1 + \tfrac{15}{5^k} & 1 - \tfrac{1}{5^k} \\ 15\left(1 - \tfrac{1}{5^k}\right) & 15 + \tfrac{1}{5^k} \end{bmatrix}.$$

This is rather like pulling a rabbit out of a hat, for we are far from having the machinery at our disposal to obtain this result; but the reader will at least be able to verify this statement by induction. From this formula we see that, the larger k becomes, the closer is the approximation

$$\begin{bmatrix} \frac{1}{4} & \frac{1}{20} \\ \frac{3}{4} & \frac{19}{20} \end{bmatrix}^k \sim \begin{bmatrix} \frac{1}{16} & \frac{1}{16} \\ \frac{15}{16} & \frac{15}{16} \end{bmatrix}.$$

Since $L_0 + M_0 = 1$ we thus have

$$\begin{bmatrix} L_k \\ M_k \end{bmatrix} \sim \begin{bmatrix} \frac{1}{16} & \frac{1}{16} \\ \frac{15}{16} & \frac{15}{16} \end{bmatrix} \begin{bmatrix} L_0 \\ M_0 \end{bmatrix} = \begin{bmatrix} \frac{1}{16} \\ \frac{15}{16} \end{bmatrix}.$$

Put another way, irrespective of the initial values of L_0 and M_0, we see that the system is 'equilibrium-seeking' in the sense that 'eventually' one sixteenth of the population remains unemployed. Of course, the lack of any notion of a limit for a sequence of matrices precludes any rigorous description of what is meant mathematically by an 'equilibrium-seeking' system. However, only the reader's intuition is called on to appreciate this particular application.

4 Difference equations

The system of equations

$$x_{n+1} = a x_n + b y_n$$
$$y_{n+1} = c x_n + d y_n$$

is called a system of *linear difference equations*. Associated with such a system are the sequences $(x_n)_{n \geq 1}$ and $(y_n)_{n \geq 1}$, and the problem is to determine the general values of x_n, y_n given initial values of x_1, y_1. The system can be written as $\mathbf{X}_{n+1} = A\mathbf{X}_n$ where

$$\mathbf{X}_n = \begin{bmatrix} x_n \\ y_n \end{bmatrix}, \quad A = \begin{bmatrix} a & b \\ c & d \end{bmatrix}.$$

Clearly, $\mathbf{X}_2 = A\mathbf{X}_1$, $\mathbf{X}_3 = A\mathbf{X}_2 = A^2\mathbf{X}_1$, and inductively we see that $\mathbf{X}_{n+1} = A^n\mathbf{X}_1$. Thus a solution can be found if an expression for A^n is known. This problem of determining the high powers of a matrix (which arose in the previous example) will be dealt with later.

5 A definition of complex numbers

Complex numbers are usually introduced at an elementary level by saying that a complex number is 'a number of the form $x + iy$ where x, y are real numbers and $i^2 = -1$'. Complex numbers add and multiply as follows :

$$(x + iy) + (x' + iy') = (x + x') + i(y + y');$$
$$(x + iy)(x' + iy') = (xx' - yy') + i(xy' + yx').$$

Also, for every real number λ we have $\lambda(x+iy) = \lambda x + i\lambda y$. This will be familiar to the reader, even though he may have little idea as to what this number system is! For example, $i = \sqrt{-1}$ is not a real number, so what does the product iy mean? Is $i0 = 0$? If so then every real number x can be written $x = x + i0$, which is familiar. This heuristic approach to complex numbers can be confusing. However, there is a simple approach that uses 2×2 matrices which is more illuminating and which we shall now describe. Of course, we have to contend with the fact that at this level the reader will be equally unsure about what a real number is, but let us proceed on the understanding that the real number system is that to which he has been accustomed throughout his schooldays.

The essential idea behind complex numbers is to develop an algebraic system of objects (called complex numbers) that is 'larger' than the real number system, in the sense that it contains a replica of this system, and in which the equation $x^2 + 1 = 0$ has a solution. This equation is, of course, insoluble in the real number system. There are several ways of 'extending' the real number system in this way and the one we shall describe uses 2×2 matrices. Consider the collection C_2 of all 2×2 matrices of the form

$$M(a, b) = \begin{bmatrix} a & b \\ -b & a \end{bmatrix},$$

where a and b are real numbers. Writing $M(a, b)$ as the sum of a symmetric matrix and a skew-symmetric matrix, we obtain

$$\begin{bmatrix} a & b \\ -b & a \end{bmatrix} = \begin{bmatrix} a & 0 \\ 0 & a \end{bmatrix} + \begin{bmatrix} 0 & b \\ -b & 0 \end{bmatrix}.$$

Thus, writing

$$J_2 = \begin{bmatrix} 0 & 1 \\ -1 & 0 \end{bmatrix},$$

we see that every such matrix $M(a, b)$ can be written

$$M(a, b) = aI_2 + bJ_2.$$

Now the collection C of all 2×2 matrices in C_2 that are of the form $aI_2 = M(a, 0)$ is a replica of the real number system; for the matrices of this type add and multiply as follows :

$$xI_2 + yI_2 = \begin{bmatrix} x+y & 0 \\ 0 & x+y \end{bmatrix} = (x+y)I_2;$$

$$xI_2 \cdot yI_2 = \begin{bmatrix} xy & 0 \\ 0 & xy \end{bmatrix} = (xy)I_2,$$

and the replication is given by associating with every real number x the matrix xI_2. Moreover, the identity matrix I_2 belongs to C, and

$$J_2^2 = \begin{bmatrix} 0 & 1 \\ -1 & 0 \end{bmatrix}\begin{bmatrix} 0 & 1 \\ -1 & 0 \end{bmatrix} = \begin{bmatrix} -1 & 0 \\ 0 & -1 \end{bmatrix} = -I_2$$

so that $J_2^2 + I_2 = 0$. In other words, in the system C the equation $x^2 + 1 = 0$ has a solution (namely J_2).

The usual notation $x + iy$ for complex numbers can be derived from C_2 by writing aI_2 as a, J_2 as i, and then $aI_2 + bJ_2$ as $a + bi$. The most remarkable feature of the complex number system is that $every$ equation of the form

$$a_n X^n + a_{n-1} X^{n-1} + \cdots + a_1 X + a_0 = 0$$

has a solution.

CHAPTER THREE

Systems of linear equations

We shall now consider in detail a systematic method of solving systems of linear equations. In working with such systems, there are three basic operations involved, namely

(1) interchanging two equations (usually for convenience);
(2) multiplying an equation by a non-zero scalar;
(3) forming a new equation by adding one equation to another.

Note that the subtraction of one equation from another can be achieved by applying (2) with the scalar equal to -1 then applying (3).

Example To solve the system

$$\begin{aligned} y + 2z &= 1 \quad (1) \\ x - 2y + z &= 0 \quad (2) \\ 3y - 4z &= 23 \quad (3) \end{aligned}$$

we multiply equation (1) by 3 and subtract the new equation from (3) to obtain $-10z = 20$, whence $z = -2$. It follows by (1) that $y = 5$, and then by (2) that $x = 2y - z = 12$.

Example Consider the system

$$\begin{aligned} x - 2y - 4z &= 0 \quad (1) \\ -2x + 4y + 3z &= 1 \quad (2) \\ -x + 2y - z &= 1 \quad (3) \end{aligned}$$

If we add together equations (1) and (2), we obtain equation (3) which is therefore superfluous. Thus we have only two equations in three unknowns. What do we mean by a solution in this case?

Example Consider the system

$$
\begin{array}{rcl}
x + y + \ z + \ t &= 1 & (1) \\
x - y - \ z + \ t &= 3 & (2) \\
-x - y + \ z - \ t &= 1 & (3) \\
-3x + y - 3z - 3t &= 4 & (4)
\end{array}
$$

Adding equations (1) and (2), we obtain $x + t = 2$, whence it follows that $y + z = -1$. Adding equations (1) and (3), we obtain $z = 1$ and consequently $y = -2$. Substituting in (4), we obtain $-3x - 3t = 9$ so that $x + t = -3$, which is not consistent with $x + t = 2$. This system therefore does not have a solution.

The above three examples were chosen to provoke the question : is there a *systematic* method of tackling systems of linear equations that avoids the haphazard manipulation of the equations, that will yield all the solutions when they exist, and make it clear when no solution is possible? The objective in this chapter is to provide a complete answer to this question.

We note first that in dealing with linear equations the 'unknowns' play a secondary role. It is in fact the coefficients (usually integers) that are important. Indeed, the system is completely determined by its augmented matrix. In order to work solely with this, we consider the following *elementary row operations* on this matrix :

(1) interchange two rows;
(2) multiply a row by a non-zero scalar;
(3) add one row to another.

These elementary row operations clearly correspond to the basic operations listed previously. It is important to observe that *these operations do not affect the solutions (if any) of the system.* In fact, if the original system of equations has a solution then this solution is also a solution of the system obtained by applying any of (1), (2), (3); and since we can in each case perform the 'inverse' operation and thereby obtain the original system, the converse is also true.

We begin by showing that elementary row operations have a fundamental interpretation in terms of matrix products.

3.1 Theorem *Let P be the $m \times m$ matrix that is obtained from I_m by permuting its rows in some way. Then for any $m \times n$*

matrix A the matrix PA is the matrix obtained from A by permuting its rows in precisely the same way.

Proof Suppose that the i-th row of P is the j-th row of I_m. Then we have $[P]_{ik} = \delta_{jk}$ for $k = 1, \ldots, m$. Consequently, for every value of k,

$$[PA]_{ik} = \sum_{t=1}^{m} [P]_{it}[A]_{tk} = \sum_{t=1}^{m} \delta_{jt}[A]_{tk} = [A]_{jk},$$

whence we see that the i-th row of PA is the j-th row of A. $\diamond$

Example The matrix

$$P = \begin{bmatrix} 1 & 0 & 0 & 0 \\ 0 & 0 & 1 & 0 \\ 0 & 1 & 0 & 0 \\ 0 & 0 & 0 & 1 \end{bmatrix}$$

is obtained from I_4 by permuting the second and third rows. If we compute the product

$$PA = \begin{bmatrix} 1 & 0 & 0 & 0 \\ 0 & 0 & 1 & 0 \\ 0 & 1 & 0 & 0 \\ 0 & 0 & 0 & 1 \end{bmatrix} \begin{bmatrix} a_1 & b_1 \\ a_2 & b_2 \\ a_3 & b_3 \\ a_4 & b_4 \end{bmatrix} = \begin{bmatrix} a_1 & b_1 \\ a_3 & b_3 \\ a_2 & b_2 \\ a_4 & b_4 \end{bmatrix}$$

we see that the effect of multiplying A on the left by P is to permute the second and third rows of A.

3.2 Theorem *Let A be an $m \times n$ matrix and let*

$$D = \begin{bmatrix} \lambda_1 & & & \\ & \lambda_2 & & \\ & & \ddots & \\ & & & \lambda_m \end{bmatrix}$$

be an $m \times m$ diagonal matrix. Then DA is the matrix obtained from A by multiplying the i-th row of A by λ_i for $i = 1, \ldots, m$.

Proof Clearly, we have $[D]_{ij} = \lambda_i \delta_{ij}$. Consequently,

$$[DA]_{ij} = \sum_{t=1}^m [D]_{it}[A]_{tj} = \sum_{t=1}^m \lambda_i \delta_{it}[A]_{tj} = \lambda_i[A]_{ij}$$

and so the i-th row of DA is simply λ_i times the i-th row of A. $\diamond$

Example If

$$D = \begin{bmatrix} 1 & 0 & 0 & 0 \\ 0 & \alpha & 0 & 0 \\ 0 & 0 & \beta & 0 \\ 0 & 0 & 0 & 1 \end{bmatrix}$$

i.e. D is obtained from I_4 by multiplying the second row of I_4 by α and the third row by β, then computing the product

$$DA = \begin{bmatrix} 1 & 0 & 0 & 0 \\ 0 & \alpha & 0 & 0 \\ 0 & 0 & \beta & 0 \\ 0 & 0 & 0 & 1 \end{bmatrix} \begin{bmatrix} a_1 & b_1 \\ a_2 & b_2 \\ a_3 & b_3 \\ a_4 & b_4 \end{bmatrix} = \begin{bmatrix} a_1 & b_1 \\ \alpha a_2 & \alpha b_2 \\ \beta a_3 & \beta b_3 \\ a_4 & b_4 \end{bmatrix}$$

we see that the effect of multiplying A on the left by D is to multiply the second row of A by α and the third row by β.

3.3 Theorem *Let P be the $m \times m$ matrix that is obtained from I_m by adding λ times the s-th row to the r-th row (where r, s are fixed with $r \neq s$). Then for any $m \times n$ matrix A the matrix PA is the matrix obtained from A by adding λ times the s-th row of A to the r-th row of A.*

Proof Let E_{rs}^λ be the $m \times m$ matrix that has λ in the (r, s)-th position and 0 elsewhere. Then

$$[E_{rs}^\lambda]_{ij} = \begin{cases} \lambda & \text{if } i = r, j = s; \\ 0 & \text{otherwise.} \end{cases}$$

Since $P = I_m + E_{rs}^\lambda$ we have

$$[PA]_{ij} = [A + E_{rs}^\lambda A]_{ij}$$
$$= [A]_{ij} + \sum_{k=1}^m [E_{rs}^\lambda]_{ik}[A]_{kj}$$
$$= \begin{cases} [A]_{ij} & \text{if } i \neq r; \\ [A]_{rj} + \lambda[A]_{sj} & \text{if } i = r. \end{cases}$$

Thus we see that PA is obtained from A by adding λ times the s-th row to the r-th row. $\diamond$

Example If

$$P = \begin{bmatrix} 1 & \lambda & 0 \\ 0 & 1 & 0 \\ 0 & 0 & 1 \end{bmatrix}$$

is obtained from I_3 by adding λ times the second row to the first row then computing the product

$$PA = \begin{bmatrix} 1 & \lambda & 0 \\ 0 & 1 & 0 \\ 0 & 0 & 1 \end{bmatrix} \begin{bmatrix} a_1 & b_1 \\ a_2 & b_2 \\ a_3 & b_3 \end{bmatrix} = \begin{bmatrix} a_1 + \lambda a_2 & b_1 + \lambda b_2 \\ a_2 & b_2 \\ a_3 & b_3 \end{bmatrix}$$

we see that the effect of multiplying A on the left by P is to add λ times the second row of A to the first row.

Definition By an *elementary matrix* of size $m \times m$ we shall mean a matrix that is obtained from I_m by applying to it a single elementary row operation.

Example Using the 'punning notation' ρ_i to mean 'row i', we have the following examples of 3×3 elementary matrices :

$$\begin{bmatrix} 1 & 0 & 0 \\ 0 & 0 & 1 \\ 0 & 1 & 0 \end{bmatrix} (\rho_2 \leftrightarrow \rho_3); \qquad \begin{bmatrix} 1 & 0 & 0 \\ 0 & 2 & 0 \\ 0 & 0 & 1 \end{bmatrix} (2\rho_2);$$

$$\begin{bmatrix} 1 & 0 & 1 \\ 0 & 1 & 0 \\ 0 & 0 & 1 \end{bmatrix} (\rho_1 + \rho_3).$$

Definition In a product AB we say that B is *pre-multiplied* by A or, equivalently, that A is *post-multiplied* by B.

The following result is now an immediate consequence of 3.1, 3.2 and 3.3 :

3.4 Theorem *Any elementary row operation on an $m \times n$ matrix A can be achieved by pre-multiplying A by a suitable elementary matrix; the elementary matrix in question is precisely that obtained by applying the same elementary row operation to I_m.* ◇

Having observed this important point, let us return to the system of equations described in the matrix form $A\mathbf{x} = \mathbf{b}$. It is clear that when we perform a basic operation to these equations all we do is to perform an elementary row operation on the augmented matrix $A|\mathbf{b}$. It follows from 3.4 that performing a basic operation on the equations is therefore the same as changing the system $A\mathbf{x} = \mathbf{b}$ to the system $EA\mathbf{x} = E\mathbf{b}$ where E is some elementary matrix; and the new system $EA\mathbf{x} = E\mathbf{b}$ is equivalent to the original system $A\mathbf{x} = \mathbf{b}$ in the sense that it has the same solutions (if any). Continuing in this way, we see that to every string of k basic operations on the system $A\mathbf{x} = \mathbf{b}$ there is a string of elementary matrices $E_1, \ldots, E_k$ such that the resulting system

$$E_k \cdots E_2 E_1 A\mathbf{x} = E_k \cdots E_2 E_1 \mathbf{b}$$

(which is of the form $B\mathbf{x} = \mathbf{c}$) is equivalent to the original system.

Now the whole idea of applying matrices to solve linear equations is to obtain a simple systematic method of finding a convenient final matrix B so that the solutions (if any) of the system $B\mathbf{x} = \mathbf{c}$ can be easily found, such solutions being precisely the solutions of the original system $A\mathbf{x} = \mathbf{b}$.

Our objective now is to develop a method of doing just that. We shall insist that the method to be developed will avoid having to write down explicitly the elementary matrices involved at each stage, that it will determine automatically whether or not the given system has a solution, and that when a solution exists it will provide all the solutions. There are two main problems that we have to deal with, namely

(1) what form should the matrix B have?
(2) can our method be designed to remove all the equations that may be superfluous?

Our requirements add up to a tall order perhaps, but we shall see in due course that the method we shall describe meets all of them.

We begin by considering the following type of matrix.

Definition By a *row-echelon* (or *stairstep*) matrix we mean a matrix of the form

$$\begin{bmatrix} 0 & \ldots & 0 & \star & & & & & \\ 0 & \ldots & 0 & 0 & \ldots & 0 & \star & & \\ 0 & \ldots & 0 & 0 & \ldots & 0 & 0 & 0 & \star & \ldots \\ & & & & \ldots & & & & \\ & & & & \ldots & & & & \end{bmatrix}$$

in which every entry under the stairstep is 0, all of the entries marked $\star$ are non-zero, and all other entries are arbitrary. (Note that the stairstep comes down one row at a time.) The entries marked $\star$ will be called the *corner entries* of the stairstep.

Example The 5×8 matrix

$$\begin{bmatrix} 0 & 1 & 3 & 0 & 2 & 9 & 0 & 1 \\ 0 & 0 & 0 & 4 & 0 & 3 & 5 & 1 \\ 0 & 0 & 0 & 0 & 0 & 1 & 1 & 1 \\ 0 & 0 & 0 & 0 & 0 & 0 & 0 & 0 \\ 0 & 0 & 0 & 0 & 0 & 0 & 0 & 0 \end{bmatrix}$$

is in row-echelon form.

3.5 Theorem *Every non-zero matrix A can be transformed by means of elementary row operations to a row-echelon matrix.*

Proof Reading from the left, the first non-zero column of A contains at least one non-zero element. By a suitable change of rows if necessary, we can move the row containing this non-zero element so that it becomes the first row, thus obtaining a matrix

$$\begin{bmatrix} 0 & \ldots & 0 & b_{11} & b_{12} & \ldots & b_{1n} \\ 0 & \ldots & 0 & b_{21} & b_{22} & \ldots & b_{2n} \\ & \vdots & & \vdots & \vdots & & \vdots \\ 0 & \ldots & 0 & b_{m1} & b_{m2} & \ldots & b_{mn} \end{bmatrix}$$

in which $b_{11} \neq 0$. Now for $i = 2, 3, \ldots, n$ subtract from the i-th row b_{i1}/b_{11} times the first row. This is a combination of elementary row operations and transforms B to the matrix

$$C = \begin{bmatrix} 0 & \ldots & 0 & b_{11} & b_{12} & \ldots & b_{1n} \\ 0 & \ldots & 0 & 0 & c_{22} & \ldots & c_{2n} \\ & \vdots & & \vdots & \vdots & & \vdots \\ 0 & \ldots & 0 & 0 & c_{m2} & \ldots & c_{mn} \end{bmatrix}$$

and begins the stairstep. We now leave the first row alone and concentrate on the $(m-1) \times (n-1)$ matrix $[c_{ij}]$. Applying the above argument to this submatrix, we can extend the stairstep by one row. Clearly, after at most m applications of this argument we arrive at a row-echelon form for A. $\diamond$

The above proof yields a practical method of reducing a given matrix to row-echelon form.

Example

$$
\begin{bmatrix} 1 & 0 & 1 & 0 & 1 \\ 1 & 1 & 0 & 0 & 2 \\ 3 & 1 & 1 & 1 & 1 \\ 0 & 1 & 2 & 1 & 2 \end{bmatrix}
\longmapsto
\begin{bmatrix} 1 & 0 & 1 & 0 & 1 \\ 0 & 1 & -1 & 0 & 1 \\ 0 & 1 & -2 & 1 & -2 \\ 0 & 1 & 2 & 1 & 2 \end{bmatrix}
\begin{matrix} \\ \rho_2 - \rho_1 \\ \rho_3 - 3\rho_1 \\ \ \end{matrix}
$$

$$
\longmapsto
\begin{bmatrix} 1 & 0 & 1 & 0 & 1 \\ 0 & 1 & -1 & 0 & 1 \\ 0 & 0 & -1 & 1 & -3 \\ 0 & 0 & 3 & 1 & 1 \end{bmatrix}
\begin{matrix} \\ \\ \rho_3 - \rho_2 \\ \rho_4 - \rho_2 \end{matrix}
$$

$$
\longmapsto
\begin{bmatrix} 1 & 0 & 1 & 0 & 1 \\ 0 & 1 & -1 & 0 & 1 \\ 0 & 0 & -1 & 1 & -3 \\ 0 & 0 & 0 & 4 & -8 \end{bmatrix}
\begin{matrix} \\ \\ \\ \rho_4 + 3\rho_3 \end{matrix}
$$

It should be noted carefully that the stairstep need not reach the bottom row, as the following Example shows.

Example

$$
\begin{bmatrix} 0 & 0 & 2 \\ 1 & -1 & 1 \\ -1 & 1 & -4 \end{bmatrix}
\longmapsto
\begin{bmatrix} 1 & -1 & 1 \\ 0 & 0 & 2 \\ -1 & 1 & -4 \end{bmatrix}
\begin{matrix} \rho_1 \leftrightarrow \rho_2 \\ \\ \ \end{matrix}
$$

$$
\longmapsto
\begin{bmatrix} 1 & -1 & 1 \\ 0 & 0 & 2 \\ 0 & 0 & -3 \end{bmatrix}
\begin{matrix} \\ \\ \rho_3 + \rho_1 \end{matrix}
$$

$$
\longmapsto
\begin{bmatrix} 1 & -1 & 1 \\ 0 & 0 & 2 \\ 0 & 0 & 0 \end{bmatrix}
\begin{matrix} \\ \\ \rho_3 + \frac{3}{2}\rho_2 \end{matrix}
$$

Indeed, the stairstep can on occasions go no further than the first row :

Example

$$\begin{bmatrix} 1 & -2 & 1 \\ 2 & -4 & 2 \\ -1 & 2 & -1 \end{bmatrix} \longmapsto \begin{bmatrix} 1 & -2 & 1 \\ 0 & 0 & 0 \\ 0 & 0 & 0 \end{bmatrix} \begin{matrix} \\ \rho_2 - 2\rho_1 \\ \rho_3 + \rho_1 \end{matrix}$$

Definition By a *Hermite* (or *reduced row-echelon*) matrix we mean a row-echelon matrix every corner entry of which is 1 and every entry lying above a corner entry is 0.

A Hermite matrix thus has the general form

$$\begin{bmatrix} 0 & \cdots & 0 & 1 & & & 0 & 0 & & 0 & & 0 \\ 0 & \cdots & 0 & 0 & \cdots & 0 & 1 & 0 & & 0 & & 0 \\ 0 & \cdots & 0 & 0 & \cdots & 0 & 0 & 1 & & 0 & & 0 \\ 0 & \cdots & 0 & 0 & \cdots & 0 & 0 & 0 & \cdots & 0 & 1 & & 0 \\ 0 & \cdots & 0 & 0 & \cdots & 0 & 0 & 0 & \cdots & 0 & 0 & \cdots & 0 & 1 \\ 0 & \cdots & 0 & 0 & \cdots & 0 & 0 & 0 & \cdots & 0 & 0 & \cdots & 0 & 0 \end{bmatrix} \cdots$$

in which the unmarked entries lying above the stairstep are arbitrary.

Example The 4×9 matrix

$$\begin{bmatrix} 1 & 0 & 1 & 0 & 2 & 2 & 0 & 0 & 1 \\ 0 & 1 & 0 & 0 & 0 & 2 & 0 & 1 & 0 \\ 0 & 0 & 0 & 0 & 0 & 0 & 1 & 2 & 1 \\ 0 & 0 & 0 & 0 & 0 & 0 & 0 & 0 & 0 \end{bmatrix}$$

is a Hermite matrix.

Example I_n is a Hermite matrix.

3.6 Theorem *Every non-zero matrix A can be transformed by means of elementary row operations to a unique Hermite matrix.*

Proof Let Z be a row-echelon matrix obtained from A by the process described in 3.5. Divide each non-zero row of Z by the (non-zero) corner entry in that row. This has the effect of making all the corner entries 1. Now subtract suitable multiples of every non-zero row from every row above it to obtain a Hermite matrix.

To show that the Hermite form of a matrix is unique is a more difficult matter and we shall defer this until later, when we shall have the necessary machinery at our disposal. ◇

Notwithstanding the delay in part of the above proof, we shall agree to accept the uniqueness of a Hermite form for A and talk about *the* Hermite matrix obtained from A. We shall denote the Hermite form of A by $H(A)$.

Example

$$
\begin{bmatrix} 1 & 2 & 1 & 2 & 1 \\ 2 & 4 & 4 & 8 & 4 \\ 3 & 6 & 5 & 7 & 7 \end{bmatrix}
\longmapsto
\begin{bmatrix} 1 & 2 & 1 & 2 & 1 \\ 0 & 0 & 2 & 4 & 2 \\ 0 & 0 & 2 & 1 & 4 \end{bmatrix}
\begin{matrix} \\ \rho_2 - 2\rho_1 \\ \rho_3 - 3\rho_1 \end{matrix}
$$

$$
\longmapsto
\begin{bmatrix} 1 & 2 & 1 & 2 & 1 \\ 0 & 0 & 2 & 4 & 6 \\ 0 & 0 & 0 & -3 & 2 \end{bmatrix}
\begin{matrix} \\ \\ \rho_3 - \rho_2 \end{matrix}
\qquad \text{row-echelon}
$$

$$
\longmapsto
\begin{bmatrix} 1 & 2 & 1 & 2 & 1 \\ 0 & 0 & 1 & 2 & 3 \\ 0 & 0 & 0 & 1 & -\frac{2}{3} \end{bmatrix}
\begin{matrix} \\ \frac{1}{2}\rho_2 \\ -\frac{1}{3}\rho_3 \end{matrix}
$$

$$
\longmapsto
\begin{bmatrix} 1 & 2 & 1 & 0 & \frac{7}{3} \\ 0 & 0 & 1 & 0 & \frac{13}{3} \\ 0 & 0 & 0 & 1 & -\frac{2}{3} \end{bmatrix}
\begin{matrix} \rho_1 - 2\rho_3 \\ \rho_2 - 2\rho_3 \\ \\ \end{matrix}
$$

$$
\longmapsto
\begin{bmatrix} 1 & 2 & 0 & 0 & -2 \\ 0 & 0 & 1 & 0 & \frac{13}{3} \\ 0 & 0 & 0 & 1 & -\frac{2}{3} \end{bmatrix}
\begin{matrix} \rho_1 - \rho_2 \\ \\ \\ \end{matrix}
$$

this final matrix being the Hermite form.

As far as the problem in hand is concerned, namely the solution of $A\mathbf{x} = \mathbf{b}$, it will transpire that the Hermite form of A is the matrix B that will satisfy our requirements. In order to prove this, we have to develop some new ideas.

In what follows, given an $m \times n$ matrix $A = [a_{ij}]$, we shall use the notation

$$\mathbf{A}_i = [a_{i1}\ a_{i2}\ \ldots\ a_{in}],$$

and we shall often not distinguish this from the i-th row of A. Similarly, the i-th column of A will often be taken to be the matrix

$$\mathbf{a}_i = \begin{bmatrix} a_{1i} \\ a_{2i} \\ \vdots \\ a_{mi} \end{bmatrix}.$$

Definition By a *linear combination* of the rows (columns) of A we shall mean an expression of the form

$$\lambda_1 x_1 + \lambda_2 x_2 + \cdots + \lambda_p x_p$$

where each x_i is a row (column) of A and every λ_i is a scalar.

Definition If $x_1, \ldots, x_p$ are rows (columns) of A then we shall say that $x_1, \ldots, x_p$ are *linearly independent* if

$$\lambda_1 x_1 + \cdots + \lambda_p x_p = 0 \implies \lambda_1 = \cdots = \lambda_p = 0.$$

Put another way, the rows (columns) $x_1, \ldots, x_p$ are linearly independent if the only way that 0 can be expressed as a linear combination of $x_1, \ldots, x_p$ is the trivial way, namely

$$0 = 0x_1 + \cdots + 0x_p.$$

If $x_1, \ldots, x_p$ are not linearly independent then we say that they are *linearly dependent*.

Example In the matrix

$$A = \begin{bmatrix} 1 & 2 & 0 & 2 \\ 0 & 1 & 1 & 1 \\ 1 & 0 & 1 & 0 \end{bmatrix}$$

the columns are not linearly independent; for $\mathbf{A}_2 = \mathbf{A}_4$ and so we have $1\mathbf{A}_2 - 1\mathbf{A}_4 = \mathbf{0}$, the scalars being non-zero. However, the first three columns are linearly independent, for if $\lambda_1 \mathbf{A}_1 + \lambda_2 \mathbf{A}_2 + \lambda_3 \mathbf{A}_3 = \mathbf{0}$ then we have

$$\begin{aligned} \lambda_1 + 2\lambda_2 &= 0 \\ \lambda_2 + \lambda_3 &= 0 \\ \lambda_1 + \lambda_3 &= 0 \end{aligned}$$

from which it is easily seen that $\lambda_1 = \lambda_2 = \lambda_3 = 0$.

3.7 Theorem *If the rows (columns) $x_1, \ldots, x_p$ are linearly independent then none of them can be zero.*

Proof If say $x_i = 0$ then we could write

$$0x_1 + \cdots + 0x_{i-1} + 1x_i + 0x_{i+1} + \cdots + 0x_p = 0,$$

which is a non-trivial linear combination equal to zero, so that $x_1, \ldots, x_p$ would not be independent. $\diamond$

The next result gives a more satisfying characterization of the term 'linearly dependent'.

3.8 Theorem $x_1, \ldots, x_p$ *are linearly dependent if and only if at least one can be expressed as a linear combination of the others.*

Proof If $x_1, \ldots, x_p$ are dependent then there exist $\lambda_1, \ldots, \lambda_p$ not all zero such that

$$\lambda_1 x_1 + \cdots + \lambda_p x_p = 0.$$

Suppose that $\lambda_k \neq 0$. Then this equation can be written in the form

$$x_k = \sum_{j \neq k} \left(-\frac{\lambda_j}{\lambda_k} \right) x_j,$$

i.e. x_k is a linear combination of $x_1, \ldots, x_{k-1}, x_{k+1}, \ldots, x_p$.
Conversely, if

$$x_k = \mu_1 x_1 + \cdots + \mu_{k-1} x_{k-1} + \mu_{k+1} x_{k+1} + \cdots + \mu_p x_p$$

then this can be written

$$\mu_1 x_1 + \cdots + \mu_{k-1} x_{k-1} + (-1)x_k + \mu_{k+1} x_{k+1} + \cdots + \mu_p x_p = 0$$

where the left-hand side is a non-trivial linear combination of $x_1, \ldots, x_p$. Thus $x_1, \ldots, x_p$ are linearly dependent. $\diamond$

3.9 Corollary *The rows of a matrix are linearly dependent if and only if one can be obtained from the others by means of elementary row operations.*

Proof This is immediate from the fact that every linear combination of rows is, by its definition, obtained by a sequence of elementary row operations. $\diamond$

Definition By the *row rank* of a matrix we mean the maximum number of linearly independent rows in the matrix.

Example The matrix

$$A = \begin{bmatrix} 1 & 2 & 0 & 0 \\ 2 & 1 & -1 & 1 \\ 5 & 4 & -2 & 2 \end{bmatrix}$$

is of row rank 2. In fact, the three rows $\mathbf{A}_1, \mathbf{A}_2, \mathbf{A}_3$ are dependent since $\mathbf{A}_3 = \mathbf{A}_1 + 2\mathbf{A}_2$; but $\mathbf{A}_1, \mathbf{A}_2$ are independent since $\lambda_1 \mathbf{A}_1 + \lambda_2 \mathbf{A}_2 = \mathbf{0}$ clearly implies that $\lambda_1 = \lambda_2 = 0$.

Example I_n has row rank n.

It turns out that the row rank of the augmented matrix in the system $A\mathbf{x} = \mathbf{b}$ determines precisely how many of the equations are not superfluous, so it is important to have a simple method of determining the row rank of a matrix. The next result provides the key to obtaining such a method.

3.10 Theorem *Elementary row operations do not affect row rank.*

Proof It is clear that an interchange of two rows has no effect on the maximum number of independent rows, i.e. the row rank.

If now $\mathbf{A}_k$ is a linear combination of p rows, which may be taken as $\mathbf{A}_1, \ldots, \mathbf{A}_p$ by the above, then so is $\lambda \mathbf{A}_k$ for every non-zero λ. It therefore follows by 3.8 that multiplying a row by a non-zero scalar has no effect on the row rank.

Finally, suppose that we add the i-th row to the j-th row to obtain a new j-th row, say $\mathbf{A}_j^* = \mathbf{A}_i + \mathbf{A}_j$. Since then

$$\lambda_1 \mathbf{A}_1 + \cdots + \lambda_i \mathbf{A}_i + \cdots + \lambda_j \mathbf{A}_j^* + \cdots + \lambda_p \mathbf{A}_p$$
$$= \lambda_1 \mathbf{A}_1 + \cdots + (\lambda_i + \lambda_j)\mathbf{A}_i + \cdots + \lambda_j \mathbf{A}_j + \cdots + \lambda_p \mathbf{A}_p,$$

it is clear that if $\mathbf{A}_1, \ldots, \mathbf{A}_i, \ldots, \mathbf{A}_j, \ldots, \mathbf{A}_p$ are independent then so are $\mathbf{A}_1, \ldots, \mathbf{A}_i, \ldots, \mathbf{A}_j^*, \ldots, \mathbf{A}_p$. Thus the addition of one row to another has no effect on the row rank. $\diamond$

3.11 Corollary *If B is any row-echelon form of A then B has the same row rank as A.*

Proof The transition of A into B is obtained purely by row operations. ◊

A practical method of determining row rank now arises from the following result.

3.12 Theorem *The row rank of a matrix is the number of non-zero rows in any row-echelon form of the matrix.*

Proof Given A, let B be a row-echelon form of A. By the way in which the Hermite form $H(A)$ is obtained from B, the number of non-zero rows of $H(A)$ is the same as the number of non-zero rows of B. But in $H(A)$ each of these rows contains a corner entry 1, and these corner entries are the only entries in their respective columns. It follows, therefore, that the non-zero rows of $H(A)$ are linearly independent. The row rank of $H(A)$ is thus the number of non-zero rows of $H(A)$, whence the result follows by 3.11. ◊

At this point it is convenient to patch a hole in the fabric : the following notion will be used to establish the uniqueness of the Hermite form.

Definition A matrix B is said to be *row-equivalent* to a matrix A if B can be obtained from A by a finite sequence of elementary row operations. Equivalently, B is row-equivalent to A if there is a matrix F which is a product of elementary matrices such that $B = FA$.

Since row operations are reversible, we have that if B is row-equivalent to A then A is row-equivalent to B. The relation of being row-equivalent is then an equivalence relation on the set of $m \times n$ matrices, its transitivity resulting from the fact that if F, G are products of elementary matrices then so is FG.

3.13 Theorem *Row-equivalent matrices have the same rank.*

Proof This is immediate from 3.10. ◊

3.14 Theorem *The Hermite form of a (non-zero) matrix is unique.*

Proof It clearly suffices to prove that if A, B are $m \times n$ Hermite matrices that are row-equivalent then $A = B$. This we do by induction on the number of columns.

It is clear that the only $m \times 1$ Hermite matrix is the column matrix $[1 \ 0 \ \ldots \ 0]^t$, so the result is trivial in this case. Suppose, by way of induction, that all row-equivalent Hermite matrices of size $m \times (n-1)$ are identical and let A, B be row-equivalent Hermite matrices of size $m \times n$. Then there is a matrix F (a product of elementary matrices) such that $B = FA$. Let $\widehat{A}, \widehat{B}$ be the $m \times (n-1)$ matrices consisting of the first $n-1$ columns of A, B respectively. Then we have $\widehat{B} = F\widehat{A}$ and so $\widehat{A}, \widehat{B}$ are row-equivalent. By the induction hypothesis, therefore, we have $\widehat{A} = \widehat{B}$. The result will now follow if we can show that the n-th columns of A, B are the same. For this purpose we note that, by 3.13, A and B have the same row rank, i.e., each being Hermite, the same number of corner entries. If this row rank is r then the row rank of $\widehat{A} = \widehat{B}$ must be either r or $r-1$. In the latter case, the n-th columns of A and B consist of a corner entry 1 in the r-th row and 0 elsewhere, so these columns are equal and hence $A = B$ in this case. In the former case we deduce from $B = FA$ that, for $1 \le i \le r$,

$$(\star) \qquad [b_{i1} \ \ldots \ b_{in}] = \sum_{k=1}^{r} \lambda_k [a_{k1} \ \ldots \ a_{kn}].$$

In particular, for the matrix $\widehat{A} = \widehat{B}$ we have

$$[a_{i1} \ \ldots \ a_{i,n-1}] = [b_{i1} \ \ldots \ b_{i,n-1}] = \sum_{k=1}^{r} \lambda_k [a_{k1} \ \ldots \ a_{k,n-1}].$$

But since the first r rows of $\widehat{A}$ are independent we deduce from this that $\lambda_i = 1$ and $\lambda_k = 0$ for $k \neq i$. It now follows from $(\star)$ that

$$[b_{i1} \ \ldots \ b_{in}] = [a_{i1} \ \ldots \ a_{in}]$$

and hence that $b_{in} = a_{in}$. Thus the n-th columns of A, B coincide and so $A = B$ also in this case. $\Diamond$

The uniqueness of the Hermite form means that two given matrices are row-equivalent if and only if they have the same Hermite form. The Hermite form $H(A)$ of A is thus a particularly important 'representative' in the corresponding equivalence class of A relative to the equivalence relation of being row-equivalent.

Similar to the concept of an elementary row operation is that of an *elementary column operation*. To obtain this, we simply replace 'row' by 'column' in the definition. It should be noted immediately that column operations cannot be used in the same way as row operations to solve systems of equations since they do not produce an equivalent system. Nevertheless, there are results concerning column operations that are 'dual' to those concerning row operations. This is because column operations on a matrix are simply row operations on the transpose of the matrix. For example, from the column analogues of 3.1, 3.2 and 3.3 (proved by transposition) we deduce the following analogue of 3.4 : *an elementary column operation on an $m \times n$ matrix can be achieved by post-multiplying the matrix by a suitable elementary matrix, namely that obtained from I_n by applying to I_n precisely the same column operation*. We define the *column rank* of a matrix to be the maximum number of independent columns. Column rank is invariant under column operations (the dual of 3.10). Furthermore, since column operations can have no effect on the independence of rows, it follows that column operations have no effect on row rank. We can therefore assert :

3.15 Theorem *Both row and column rank are invariant with respect to both row and column operations.* ◇

We now ask whether there is any connection between the row rank and the column rank; i.e. whether the maximum number of independent rows is connected in any way with the maximum number of independent columns. The answer is perhaps surprising :

3.16 Theorem *Row rank and column rank are the same.*

Proof Given the non-zero $m \times n$ matrix A we know that A and $H(A)$ have the same row rank, p say, and we can apply column operations to $H(A)$ without changing this row rank. Also, A and $H(A)$ have the same column rank (since row operations do not affect column rank). Now by a suitable re-arrangement of its columns $H(A)$ can be transformed into the form

$$\begin{bmatrix} I_p & ? \\ 0 & 0 \end{bmatrix},$$

in which the submatrix marked ? is unknown but can be reduced to 0 by further column operations using the first p columns. Thus $H(A)$ can be transformed into the form

$$\begin{bmatrix} I_p & 0 \\ 0 & 0 \end{bmatrix}.$$

Now by its construction this matrix has the row rank and the column rank of A. But clearly the row rank and the column rank are each equal to p. It therefore follows that the row rank of A is the column rank of A. $\Diamond$

Because of 3.16 we shall talk simply of the *rank* of a matrix and shall mean by this either the row rank or the column rank, whichever is appropriate.

We now have to hand enough machinery to solve our problem. This is dealt with in the following three results.

3.17 Theorem *If A is an $m \times n$ matrix then the homogeneous system $Ax = 0$ has a non-trivial solution if and only if the rank of A is less than n.*

Proof Let a_i denote the i-th column of A. Then there is a non-zero column matrix

$$x = \begin{bmatrix} x_1 \\ x_2 \\ \vdots \\ x_n \end{bmatrix}$$

such that $Ax = 0$ if and only if there are scalars $x_1, \ldots, x_n$ which are not all zero and such that

$$x_1 a_1 + x_2 a_2 + \cdots + x_n a_n = 0;$$

for, as is readily seen, the left-hand side of this equation is simply Ax. Hence a non-trivial (=non-zero) solution x exists if and only if the columns of A are linearly dependent. Since A has a total of n columns, this is the case if and only if the (column) rank of A is less than n. $\Diamond$

3.18 Theorem *A non-homogeneous system* $A\mathbf{x} = \mathbf{b}$ *has a solution if and only if the rank of the coefficient matrix is equal to the rank of the augmented matrix.*

Proof If A is of size $m \times n$ then there is an $n \times 1$ matrix $\mathbf{x}$ such that $A\mathbf{x} = \mathbf{b}$ if and only if there are scalars $x_1, \ldots, x_n$ such that

$$x_1 \mathbf{a}_1 + x_2 \mathbf{a}_2 + \cdots + x_n \mathbf{a}_n = \mathbf{b}.$$

This is the case if and only if $\mathbf{b}$ is linearly dependent on the columns of A, which is the case if and only if the augmented matrix is column-equivalent to A, i.e. has the same (column) rank as A. $\Diamond$

Definition We shall say that a system of equations is *consistent* if it has a solution (which, in the homogeneous case, is non-trivial); otherwise, we shall say that it is *inconsistent*.

3.19 Theorem *Let a consistent system of linear equations have as coefficient matrix the $m \times n$ matrix A. If the rank of A is p then $n - p$ of the unknowns can be assigned arbitrarily and the equations solved in terms of them as parameters.*

Proof Working with the augmented matrix $A|\mathbf{b}$, or simply with A in the homogeneous case, perform row operations to transform A to Hermite form. We thus obtain a matrix $H(A)|\mathbf{c}$ in which, if the rank of A is p, there are p non-zero rows. The corresponding system of equations $H(A)\mathbf{x} = \mathbf{c}$ is equivalent to the original system, and its form allows us to assign $n - p$ of the unknowns as solution parameters. $\Diamond$

The last statement in the above proof depends on the form of $H(A)$. The assignment of unknowns as solution parameters is best illustrated by examples. This we shall now do. It should be noted that in practice there is no need to first test for consistency using 3.18; the method of solution will determine this automatically.

Example Let us determine for what values of α the system

$$\begin{aligned}
x + y + z &= 1 \\
2x - y + 2z &= 1 \\
x + 2y + z &= \alpha
\end{aligned}$$

has a solution. A solution exists if and only if the rank of the coefficient matrix is the same as the rank of the augmented matrix (3.18), these ranks being determined by the number of non-zero rows in any row-echelon form (3.12). So we reduce the augmented matrix to row-echelon form :

$$
\begin{bmatrix} 1 & 1 & 1 & 1 \\ 2 & -1 & 2 & 1 \\ 1 & 2 & 1 & \alpha \end{bmatrix} \longmapsto \begin{bmatrix} 1 & 1 & 1 & 1 \\ 0 & -3 & 0 & -1 \\ 0 & 1 & 0 & \alpha - 1 \end{bmatrix}
$$

$$
\longmapsto \begin{bmatrix} 1 & 1 & 1 & 1 \\ 0 & 1 & 0 & \frac{1}{3} \\ 0 & 1 & 0 & \alpha - 1 \end{bmatrix}
$$

$$
\longmapsto \begin{bmatrix} 1 & 1 & 1 & 1 \\ 0 & 1 & 0 & \frac{1}{3} \\ 0 & 0 & 0 & \alpha - \frac{4}{3} \end{bmatrix} .
$$

It is now clear that the ranks are the same (and hence a solution exists) if and only if $\alpha = \frac{4}{3}$. In this case the rank is 2 and from the form of the Hermite matrix we can read off the solution, namely

$$
y = \frac{1}{3}
$$
$$
x = \frac{2}{3} - z
$$

for arbitrary z.

Example Consider now the system

$$
\begin{aligned}
x + y + z + t &= 4 \\
x + \beta y + z + t &= 4 \\
x + y + \beta z + (3 - \beta)t &= 6 \\
2x + 2y + 2z + \beta t &= 6
\end{aligned}
$$

The augmented matrix is

$$
\begin{bmatrix} 1 & 1 & 1 & 1 & 4 \\ 1 & \beta & 1 & 1 & 4 \\ 1 & 1 & \beta & 3 - \beta & 6 \\ 2 & 2 & 2 & \beta & 6 \end{bmatrix}
$$

which can be reduced to row-echelon form by means of the row operations $\rho_2 - \rho_1, \rho_3 - \rho_1, \rho_4 - 2\rho_1$. We obtain

$$(\star) \qquad \begin{bmatrix} 1 & 1 & 1 & 1 & 4 \\ 0 & \beta-1 & 0 & 0 & 0 \\ 0 & 0 & \beta-1 & 2-\beta & 2 \\ 0 & 0 & 0 & \beta-2 & -2 \end{bmatrix}.$$

Now if $\beta \neq 1, 2$ then the rank of the coefficient matrix is clearly 4, as is that of the augmented matrix. By 3.19, therefore, a unique solution exists (there are no unknowns that we can assign as solution parameters). To find the solution, we transform the above row-echelon matrix to Hermite form :

$$\longmapsto \begin{bmatrix} 1 & 1 & 1 & 1 & 4 \\ 0 & 1 & 0 & 0 & 0 \\ 0 & 0 & 1 & \frac{2-\beta}{\beta-1} & \frac{2}{\beta-1} \\ 0 & 0 & 0 & 1 & \frac{-2}{\beta-2} \end{bmatrix}$$

$$\longmapsto \begin{bmatrix} 1 & 1 & 1 & 1 & 4 \\ 0 & 1 & 0 & 0 & 0 \\ 0 & 0 & 1 & 0 & 0 \\ 0 & 0 & 0 & 1 & \frac{-2}{\beta-2} \end{bmatrix}$$

$$\longmapsto \begin{bmatrix} 1 & 0 & 0 & 0 & 4+\frac{2}{\beta-2} \\ 0 & 1 & 0 & 0 & 0 \\ 0 & 0 & 1 & 0 & 0 \\ 0 & 0 & 0 & 1 & \frac{-2}{\beta-2} \end{bmatrix}.$$

The system of equations that corresponds to this is

$$\begin{aligned} x & = 4+\tfrac{2}{\beta-2} \\ y & = 0 \\ z & = 0 \\ t & = \tfrac{-2}{\beta-2} \end{aligned}$$

which gives the solution immediately.

Consider now the exceptional values. First let $\beta = 2$. Then the matrix $(\star)$ becomes

$$\begin{bmatrix} 1 & 1 & 1 & 1 & 4 \\ 0 & 1 & 0 & 0 & 0 \\ 0 & 0 & 1 & 0 & 2 \\ 0 & 0 & 0 & 0 & -2 \end{bmatrix},$$

and in the system of equations that corresponds to this augmented matrix the final equation is

$$0x + 0y + 0z + 0t = -2,$$

which is impossible. Thus when $\beta = 2$ the system is inconsistent.

If now $\beta = 1$ the matrix $(\star)$ becomes

$$\begin{bmatrix} 1 & 1 & 1 & 1 & 4 \\ 0 & 0 & 0 & 0 & 0 \\ 0 & 0 & 0 & 1 & 2 \\ 0 & 0 & 0 & -1 & -2 \end{bmatrix}$$

which transforms to the Hermite form

$$\begin{bmatrix} 1 & 1 & 1 & 0 & 2 \\ 0 & 0 & 0 & 1 & 2 \\ 0 & 0 & 0 & 0 & 0 \\ 0 & 0 & 0 & 0 & 0 \end{bmatrix}.$$

The system of equations corresponding to this is

$$x + y + z = 2$$
$$t = 2$$

Here the coefficient matrix is of rank 2 and so we can assign $4 - 2 = 2$ of the unknowns as solution parameters. We can therefore take as the solution

$$x = 2 - y - z$$
$$t = 2$$

where y, z are arbitrary.

CHAPTER FOUR

Invertible matrices

In 1.3 we showed that every $m \times n$ matrix A has an additive inverse, denoted by $-A$, which is the unique $m \times n$ matrix X such that $A + X = 0$. In this Chapter we consider the multiplicative analogue of this for square matrices.

Definition Let A be an $n \times n$ matrix. Then an $n \times n$ matrix X is said to be a *left inverse* of A if $XA = I_n$; and a *right inverse* of A if $AX = I_n$.

Despite the fact that matrix multiplication is in general non-commutative, we have the following result.

4.1 Theorem *If the $n \times n$ matrix A has a left inverse X and a right inverse Y then $X = Y$.*

Proof Since $XA = I_n = AY$ we have $X = XI_n = X(AY) = (XA)Y = I_nY = Y$. $\diamondsuit$

Can a square matrix have a left inverse but no right inverse? The answer to this question is, perhaps surprisingly, no. Indeed, the existence of a left inverse implies the existence of a right inverse (and vice-versa) and, by 4.1, these inverses coincide. We establish this fact in the following result.

4.2 Theorem *If A is an $n \times n$ matrix then the following statements are equivalent :*

(1) *A has a left inverse;*
(2) *A has a right inverse;*
(3) *A is of rank n;*
(4) *the Hermite form of A is I_n;*
(5) *A is a product of elementary matrices.*

Proof We prove the equivalence of the five statements by establishing the following logical implications :

$$(2) \Rightarrow (3) \Rightarrow (4) \Rightarrow (1) \Rightarrow (2) \quad \text{and} \quad (3) \Leftrightarrow (5).$$

$(2) \Rightarrow (3)$: Suppose that A has a right inverse Y. Then $AY = I_n$ and this equation can be expanded into the n equations

$$(i = 1, \ldots, n) \qquad A\mathbf{y}_i = \delta_i$$

where δ_i denotes the i-th column of I_n. By 3.18 we have, for every i,

$$\text{rank } A = \text{rank } A|\delta_i.$$

Since $\delta_1, \ldots, \delta_n$ are linearly independent, it follows that

$$\text{rank } A = \text{rank } A|\delta_1 = \text{rank } A|\delta_1|\delta_2 = \cdots = \text{rank } A|I_n = n.$$

$(3) \Rightarrow (4)$: If A is of rank n then the Hermite form of A must have n non-zero rows, hence n corner entries 1. The only possibility is I_n.

$(4) \Rightarrow (1)$: If the Hermite form of A is I_n then there is a finite string of elementary matrices $E_1, \ldots, E_k$ (representing row operations) such that

$$E_k \cdots E_2 E_1 A = I_n.$$

It follows that A has a left inverse, namely $X = E_k \cdots E_2 E_1$.

$(1) \Rightarrow (2)$: Suppose that X is a left inverse of A, so that $XA = I_n$. Then X has a right inverse (namely A). Since we have shown that $(2) \Rightarrow (1)$, it follows that X also has a left inverse. By 4.1, this left inverse must be A and so we have $AX = I_n$ so that X is also a right inverse of A.

$(3) \Rightarrow (5)$: If A is of rank n then, since $(3) \Rightarrow (1)$, A has a left inverse X. Since $XA = I_n$ we see that X has a right inverse A and so, since $(2) \Rightarrow (4)$, there is a string of elementary matrices $F_1, \ldots, F_q$ that reduce X to I_n in the sense that $F_q \cdots F_2 F_1 X = I_n$. Consequently we have

$$A = I_n A = (F_q \cdots F_1 X)A = F_q \cdots F_1(XA) = F_q \cdots F_1$$

and so A is a product of elementary matrices.

$(5) \Rightarrow (3)$: Suppose that $A = E_1 \cdots E_p$ where each E_i is an elementary matrix. Now E_p is of rank n since it is obtained from I_n by an elementary operation, which does not alter the rank. Also, multiplication by an elementary matrix is equivalent to an elementary operation, which leaves the rank the same as before. It follows, therefore, that the rank of the product $E_1 \cdots E_p$ is the rank of E_p, which is n. Thus the rank of A is n. $\diamondsuit$

It is immediate from the above important result that if an $n \times n$ matrix A has a one-sided inverse then this is a two-sided inverse; moreover, by 4.1, it is unique. We denote the unique inverse of A (when it exists) by A^{-1}. If A has an inverse then we say that A is *invertible*. It is clear that if A is an invertible matrix then so is A^{-1} : since $AA^{-1} = I_n = A^{-1}A$ and inverses are unique, we deduce that $(A^{-1})^{-1} = A$.

We note at this juncture that by 4.2 we can assert that B is row-equivalent to A if and only if there is an invertible matrix F such that $B = FA$.

Another useful feature of 4.2 is that it provides a relatively simple method of determining whether or not the inverse of A exists, and of computing A^{-1} when it does exist. This method consists of transforming A to Hermite form : if this turns out to be I_n then A has an inverse, this being given by the product of the elementary matrices used [recall the proof of $(4) \Rightarrow (1)$ above]; and if the Hermite form is not I_n then the matrix has no inverse. It is important to note that in practice there is no need to determine the elementary matrices involved at each stage. We simply begin with the array $A \,|\, I_n$ and, each time we apply an elementary row operation to A, we apply the same row operation to the matrix on the right of A. In this way we obtain a sequence of stages which we can represent as

$$A|I_n \longmapsto E_1A|E_1 \longmapsto E_2E_1A|E_2E_1 \longmapsto \cdots.$$

At every stage in the reduction we have an array of the form $S|Q$ where $S = E_i \cdots E_2E_1A$ and $Q = E_i \cdots E_2E_1$, so that $QA = S$. If A has an inverse then the final configuration will be $I_n|E_p \cdots E_1$ so that $E_p \cdots E_1A = I_n$ and hence $A^{-1} = E_p \cdots E_1$.

Example Consider the matrix

$$\begin{bmatrix} 1 & 2 & 3 \\ 1 & 3 & 4 \\ 1 & 4 & 4 \end{bmatrix}.$$

Applying the above procedure, we obtain

$$
\left[\begin{array}{ccc|ccc} 1 & 2 & 3 & 1 & 0 & 0 \\ 1 & 3 & 4 & 0 & 1 & 0 \\ 1 & 4 & 4 & 0 & 0 & 1 \end{array}\right]
\longmapsto
\left[\begin{array}{ccc|ccc} 1 & 2 & 3 & 1 & 0 & 0 \\ 0 & 1 & 1 & -1 & 1 & 0 \\ 0 & 2 & 1 & -1 & 0 & 1 \end{array}\right]
$$

$$
\longmapsto
\left[\begin{array}{ccc|ccc} 1 & 2 & 3 & 1 & 0 & 0 \\ 0 & 1 & 1 & -1 & 1 & 0 \\ 0 & 0 & -1 & 1 & -2 & 1 \end{array}\right]
$$

$$
\longmapsto
\left[\begin{array}{ccc|ccc} 1 & 2 & 3 & 1 & 0 & 0 \\ 0 & 1 & 0 & 0 & -1 & 1 \\ 0 & 0 & -1 & 1 & -2 & 1 \end{array}\right]
$$

$$
\longmapsto
\left[\begin{array}{ccc|ccc} 1 & 2 & 0 & 4 & -6 & 3 \\ 0 & 1 & 0 & 0 & -1 & 1 \\ 0 & 0 & -1 & 1 & -2 & 1 \end{array}\right]
$$

$$
\longmapsto
\left[\begin{array}{ccc|ccc} 1 & 0 & 0 & 4 & -4 & 1 \\ 0 & 1 & 0 & 0 & -1 & 1 \\ 0 & 0 & 1 & -1 & 2 & -1 \end{array}\right]
$$

so A has an inverse, namely

$$A^{-1} = \begin{bmatrix} 4 & -4 & 1 \\ 0 & -1 & 1 \\ -1 & 2 & -1 \end{bmatrix}.$$

We shall see later other methods of finding inverses of square matrices. For the present, we consider some further results concerning inverses. First we note that if A, B are invertible $n \times n$ matrices then $A + B$ is not invertible in general. For example, take $A = I_n$ and $B = -I_n$ and observe that the zero $n \times n$ matrix is not invertible. However, as the following result shows, products of invertible matrices are invertible.

4.3 Theorem *Let A, B be $n \times n$ matrices. If A and B are invertible then so is AB; moreover, $(AB)^{-1} = B^{-1}A^{-1}$.*

Proof It suffices to observe that

$$ABB^{-1}A^{-1} = AI_nA^{-1} = AA^{-1} = I_n$$

whence $B^{-1}A^{-1}$ is a right inverse of AB. By 4.2, this is then the inverse of AB. Thus AB is invertible with $(AB)^{-1} = B^{-1}A^{-1}$. $\diamond$

4.4 Corollary *If A is invertible then so is A^m for every positive integer m; moreover, $(A^m)^{-1} = (A^{-1})^m$.*

Proof The result is trivial for $m = 1$. Suppose, by way of induction, that it holds for m. Then by 4.3 we have

$$(A^{-1})^{m+1} = A^{-1}(A^{-1})^m = A^{-1}(A^m)^{-1} = (A^{m+1})^{-1}$$

so it holds for $m + 1$. $\diamond$

4.5 Theorem *If A is invertible then so is its transpose; we have $(A^t)^{-1} = (A^{-1})^t$.*

Proof By 4.3 we have

$$I_n = I_n^t = (AA^{-1})^t = (A^{-1})^t A^t$$

and so $(A^{-1})^t$ is a left inverse of A^t, whence it is the inverse of A^t. $\diamond$

Recall that an $n \times n$ matrix A is said to be *orthogonal* if it is such that $AA^t = I_n = A^tA$. By 4.2 we see that only one of these equalities is necessary. An orthogonal matrix is thus one whose inverse exists and is the transpose.

Example A 2×2 matrix is orthogonal if and only if it is of one of the forms

$$\begin{bmatrix} a & b \\ -b & a \end{bmatrix}, \qquad \begin{bmatrix} a & b \\ b & -a \end{bmatrix}$$

in which $a^2 + b^2 = 1$. In fact, from

$$\begin{bmatrix} a & b \\ c & d \end{bmatrix}\begin{bmatrix} a & c \\ b & d \end{bmatrix} = \begin{bmatrix} 1 & 0 \\ 0 & 1 \end{bmatrix}$$

we obtain $a^2 + b^2 = 1, ac + bd = 0, c^2 + d^2 = 1$. The first two equations show that if $a = 0$ then $d = 0$, and the second and third equations show that if $d = 0$ then $a = 0$. Now when $a = d = 0$ the equations give $b = \pm 1, c = \pm 1$. On the other hand, when a, d are not zero the middle equation gives $c/d = -(b/a)$ so either $c = -b, d = a$ or $c = b, d = -a$. It then follows that in all cases the matrix is of one of the stated forms. Note that in the above forms the matrix on the left is a rotation matrix (take $a = \cos \vartheta$ and $b = \sin \vartheta$).

If P, A are $n \times n$ matrices with P invertible then it is easy to prove by induction that, for all positive integers m,

$$(P^{-1}AP)^m = P^{-1}A^m P.$$

In fact, this is trivial for $m = 1$; and the inductive step follows from

$$(P^{-1}AP)^{m+1} = (P^{-1}AP)(P^{-1}AP)^m$$
$$= P^{-1}APP^{-1}A^m P$$
$$= P^{-1}A^{m+1}P.$$

Now in certain applications it is important to be able to find an invertible matrix P such that $P^{-1}AP$ is of a particularly simple form. Consider, for example, the case where P can be found such that $P^{-1}AP$ is a *diagonal* matrix D. Then from the above formula we have $D^m = P^{-1}A^m P$ and consequently $A^m = PD^m P^{-1}$. Since D^m is easy to compute for a diagonal matrix D (simply take the m-th power of the diagonal entries), it is then an easy matter to compute A^m. The problem of computing high powers of a matrix is one that we have seen before, in the 'equilibrium-seeking' example in Chapter Two, and this is precisely the method that is used to compute A^k in that example. Of course, how to determine precisely when we can find an invertible matrix P such that $P^{-1}AP$ is a diagonal matrix (or some other 'nice' matrix) is quite another problem. A similar problem consists of finding under what conditions there exists an orthogonal matrix P such that $P^t AP$ is diagonal. Why we should wish to be able to do this, and how to do it, are two of the most important questions in the whole of linear algebra. A full answer is very deep and has remarkable implications on both the theoretical and practical sides.

CHAPTER FIVE

Vector spaces

In order to proceed further with matrices we have to take a wider view of matters. This we do through the following important notion.

Definition By a *vector space* we shall mean a set V on which there are defined two operations, one called addition and the other called multiplication by scalars, such that the following properties hold :

(V_1) $x + y = y + x$ for all $x, y \in V$;

(V_2) $(x + y) + z = x + (y + z)$ for all $x, y, z \in V$;

(V_3) there exists an element $0 \in V$ such that $x + 0 = x$ for all $x \in V$;

(V_4) for every $x \in V$ there exists an element $-x \in V$ such that $x + (-x) = 0$;

(V_5) $\lambda(x + y) = \lambda x + \lambda y$ for all $x, y \in V$ and all scalars λ;

(V_6) $(\lambda + \mu)x = \lambda x + \mu x$ for all $x \in V$ and all scalars λ, μ;

(V_7) $(\lambda\mu)x = \lambda(\mu x)$ for all $x \in V$ and all scalars λ, μ;

(V_8) $1x = x$ for all $x \in V$.

When the scalars are all real numbers, we shall often talk of a *real* vector space; and when the scalars are all complex numbers we shall talk of a *complex* vector space.

Example Let $\mathrm{Mat}_{m \times n}(\mathbb{R})$ be the set of all $m \times n$ matrices with real entries. Then by 1.1, 1.2, 1.3, 1.4 we see that $\mathrm{Mat}_{m \times n}(\mathbb{R})$ is a real vector space under the usual addition of matrices and multiplication by scalars.

Example The set $\mathbb{R}^n$ of n-tuples $(x_1, \ldots, x_n)$ of real numbers is a real vector space under the following component-wise definitions of addition and multiplication by scalars :

$$(x_1, \ldots, x_n) + (y_1, \ldots, y_n) = (x_1 + y_1, \ldots, x_n + y_n),$$
$$\lambda(x_1, \ldots, x_n) = (\lambda x_1, \ldots, \lambda x_n).$$

Geometrically, $\mathbb{R}^2$ represents the cartesian plane, and $\mathbb{R}^3$ represents three-dimensional cartesian space.

Similarly, the set $\mathbb{C}^n$ of n-tuples of complex numbers can be made into both a real vector space (real scalars) and a complex vector space (complex scalars).

Example Let Map$(\mathbb{R}, \mathbb{R})$ be the set of all mappings $f : \mathbb{R} \to \mathbb{R}$. For two such mappings f, g define $f + g : \mathbb{R} \to \mathbb{R}$ by the prescription $(f + g)(x) = f(x) + g(x)$ for every $x \in \mathbb{R}$, and define $\lambda f : \mathbb{R} \to \mathbb{R}$ for every $\lambda \in \mathbb{R}$ by the prescription $(\lambda f)(x) = \lambda f(x)$ for every $x \in \mathbb{R}$. Then these operations of addition and multiplication by scalars make Map$(\mathbb{R}, \mathbb{R})$ into a real vector space.

Example Let $\mathbb{R}_{n+1}[X]$ be the set of polynomials of degree at most n with real coefficients. Define addition by setting

$$(a_0 + a_1 X + \cdots + a_n X^n) + (b_0 + b_1 X + \cdots + b_n X^n)$$
$$= (a_0 + b_0) + (a_1 + b_1)X + \cdots + (a_n + b_n)X^n$$

and a multiplication by scalars by setting

$$\lambda(a_0 + a_1 X + \cdots + a_n X^n) = \lambda a_0 + \lambda a_1 X + \cdots + \lambda a_n X^n.$$

Then $\mathbb{R}_{n+1}[X]$ has the structure of a real vector space.

It should be noted that in the definition of a vector space the scalars need not be restricted to be real or complex numbers. They can in fact belong to any 'field' F. Although in what follows we shall find it convenient to say that 'V is a vector space over a field F' to indicate that the scalars come from a field F, we shall in fact assume throughout that F is either the field $\mathbb{R}$ of real numbers or the field $\mathbb{C}$ of complex numbers.

We now list some basic properties of the multiplication by scalars in a vector space that follow from the above axioms. We shall denote, at least for a while, the additive identity element of V by 0_V and that of F (i.e. $\mathbb{R}$ or $\mathbb{C}$) by 0_F.

5.1 Theorem *If V is a vector space over a field F then*

(1) $\lambda 0_V = 0_V$ *for every* $\lambda \in F$;

(2) $0_F x = 0_V$ *for every* $x \in V$;

(3) *if* $\lambda x = 0_V$ *then either* $\lambda = 0_F$ *or* $x = 0_V$;

(4) $(-\lambda)x = -(\lambda x) = \lambda(-x)$ *for all* $x \in V$ *and* $\lambda \in F$.

Proof (1) By (V_3) and (V_5) we have $\lambda 0_V = \lambda(0_V + 0_V) = \lambda 0_V + \lambda 0_V$; now add $-\lambda 0_V$ to each side.

(2) By (V_6) we have $0_F x = (0_F + 0_F)x = 0_F x + 0_F x$; now add $-0_F x$ to each side.

(3) Suppose that $\lambda x = 0_V$ and that $\lambda \neq 0_F$. Then λ has a multiplicative inverse λ^{-1} and so, by (V_7) and (1),

$$x = 1_F x = (\lambda^{-1}\lambda)x = \lambda^{-1}(\lambda x) = \lambda^{-1}0_V = 0_V.$$

(4) By (2) and (V_6), $0_V = [\lambda + (-\lambda)]x = \lambda x + (-\lambda)x$; now add $-\lambda x$ to each side.

Also, by (1) and (V_5), $0_V = \lambda[x + (-x)] = \lambda x + \lambda(-x)$; now add $-\lambda x$ to each side. $\diamond$

The reader should pause to verify the various items in 5.1 in the particular case of the vector space $\text{Mat}_{m \times n}(\mathbb{R})$.

In order to study vector spaces we begin by concentrating on the substructures, i.e. those subsets that are also vector spaces.

Definition Let V be a vector space over a field F. By a *subspace* of V we mean a non-empty subset W of V that is closed under the operations of V, in the sense that

(1) if $x, y \in W$ then $x + y \in W$;

(2) if $x \in W$ and $\lambda \in F$ then $\lambda x \in W$.

Note that (1) says that sums of elements of W belong to W, and (2) says that scalar multiples of elements of W belong to W. When these properties hold, W inherits from the parent space V all the other properties required in the definition of a vector space. For example, by taking $\lambda = -1$ in (2) we see that if $x \in W$ then $-x \in W$; and then taking $y = -x$ in (1) we obtain $0_V \in W$.

Example Every vector space V is (trivially) a subspace of itself; this is then the largest subspace of V.

Example By 5.1(1), the singleton subset $\{0_V\}$ is a subspace of V; this is the smallest subspace of V since, as observed above, we have $0_V \in W$ for every subspace W.

Example $\mathbb{R}$ is a subspace of the real vector space $\mathbb{C}$; clearly, properties (1) and (2) above hold with $W = \mathbb{R}$ and $F = \mathbb{R}$.

Example In the real vector space $\mathbb{R}^2$ the set $X = \{(x,0) \; ; \; x \in \mathbb{R}\}$ is a subspace; for $(x_1,0)+(x_2,0) = (x_1+x_2,0)$ and $\lambda(x,0) = (\lambda x,0)$ and so (1) and (2) are satisfied. This subspace is simply the 'x-axis' in the cartesian plane $\mathbb{R}^2$. Similarly, the 'y-axis' $Y = \{(0,y) \; ; \; y \in \mathbb{R}\}$ is a subspace of $\mathbb{R}^2$.

Example In the cartesian plane $\mathbb{R}^2$ every line through the origin has a description in the form of a particular subset of $\mathbb{R}^2$, namely

$$L = \{(x,y) \; ; \; \alpha x + \beta y = 0\},$$

the gradient of the line being given by $\tan \vartheta = -\alpha/\beta$. Now if $(x_1,y_1) \in L$ and $(x_2,y_2) \in L$ then $\alpha x_1 = -\beta y_1$ and $\alpha x_2 = -\beta y_2$ whence $\alpha(x_1 + x_2) = -\beta(y_1 + y_2)$ so that

$$(x_1,y_1) + (x_2,y_2) = (x_1 + x_2, y_1 + y_2) \in L;$$

and if $(x,y) \in L$ then $\alpha x = -\beta y$ gives $\alpha \lambda x = -\beta \lambda y$ for every $\lambda \in \mathbb{R}$ so that

$$\lambda(x,y) = (\lambda x, \lambda y) \in L.$$

Thus we see that every line passing through the origin is a subspace of $\mathbb{R}^2$. As we shall see later, apart from $\{(0,0)\}$ and $\mathbb{R}^2$, these are the only subspaces of $\mathbb{R}^2$.

Example In the cartesian space $\mathbb{R}^3$ every plane through the origin has a description in the form

$$P = \{(x,y,z) \; ; \; \alpha x + \beta y + \gamma z = 0\}.$$

To see the geometry of this, observe that if we fix z, say $z = k$, then 'the plane $z = k$' (i.e. the set $\{(x,y,k) \; ; \; x,y \in \mathbb{R}\}$) slices through P in the line $\{(x,y,k) \; ; \; \alpha x + \beta y = -\gamma k\}$. Now if $(x_1,y_1,z_1) \in P$ and $(x_2,y_2,z_2) \in P$ then it is readily seen that

$$(x_1,y_1,z_1) + (x_2,y_2,z_2) = (x_1 + x_2, y_1 + y_2, z_1 + z_2) \in P;$$

and if $(x, y, z) \in P$ then, for every $\lambda \in \mathbb{R}$,

$$\lambda(x, y, z) = (\lambda x, \lambda y, \lambda z) \in P.$$

Thus we see that every plane through the origin is a subspace of $\mathbb{R}^3$. We shall see later that, apart from $\{(0,0,0)\}$ and $\mathbb{R}^3$, the only subspaces of $\mathbb{R}^3$ are lines through the origin and planes through the origin.

Example An $n \times n$ matrix over a field F is said to be *lower triangular* if it is of the form

$$\begin{bmatrix} a_{11} & 0 & 0 & \cdots & 0 \\ a_{21} & a_{22} & 0 & \cdots & 0 \\ a_{31} & a_{32} & a_{33} & \cdots & 0 \\ \vdots & \vdots & \vdots & \ddots & \vdots \\ a_{n1} & a_{n2} & a_{n3} & \cdots & a_{nn} \end{bmatrix}$$

i.e. if $a_{ij} = 0$ whenever $i < j$. The set of lower triangular $n \times n$ matrices is a subspace of the vector space $\mathrm{Mat}_{n \times n}(F)$; for, if A and B are lower triangular then clearly so is $A + B$, and so also is λA.

Example The set $\mathrm{Map}(\mathbb{R}, \mathbb{R})$ of all real functions (i.e. mappings from $\mathbb{R}$ to itself) is, as we have seen, a vector space. Consider now the subset $\mathrm{Con}(\mathbb{R}, \mathbb{R})$ of all continuous functions. As is shown in courses on analysis, if f, g are continuous then so is $f + g$, and so is λf for every $\lambda \in \mathbb{R}$. Thus we see that $\mathrm{Con}(\mathbb{R}, \mathbb{R})$ is also a vector space, being a subspace of the vector space $\mathrm{Map}(\mathbb{R}, \mathbb{R})$.

Likewise, if $\mathrm{Diff}(\mathbb{R}, \mathbb{R})$ is the subset of all differentiable functions then this is also a subspace of $\mathrm{Map}(\mathbb{R}, \mathbb{R})$; for if f, g are differentiable then so is $f + g$, and so is λf for every $\lambda \in \mathbb{R}$.

As the above examples illustrate, in order to show that a given set is a vector space it is often very easy to show this by proving that it is a subspace of some well-known and considerably larger vector space.

Suppose now that A and B are subspaces of a vector space V over a field F and consider their intersection $A \cap B$. We know that $0_V \in A$ and $0_V \in B$ and so $0_V \in A \cap B$ so that $A \cap B \neq \emptyset$.

Now if $x, y \in A \cap B$ then $x, y \in A$ gives $x + y \in A$, and $x, y \in B$ gives $x + y \in B$, whence we have that $x + y \in A \cap B$. Likewise, if $x \in A \cap B$ then $x \in A$ gives $\lambda x \in A$, and $x \in B$ gives $\lambda x \in B$ for every $\lambda \in F$, whence we have that $\lambda x \in A \cap B$. Thus we see that $A \cap B$ is a subspace of V. More generally, we have :

5.2 Theorem *The intersection of any collection of subspaces of a vector space V is a subspace of V.*

Proof Let C be a collection of subspaces of V and let T be their intersection. Then $T \neq \emptyset$ since every subspace in C contains 0_V, whence so does T. Suppose now that $x, y \in T$. Since x and y then belong to every subspace W in the collection C, so does $x + y$ and hence $x + y \in T$. Also, if $x \in T$ then x belongs to every subspace W in the collection C, whence so does λx for every λ, and so $\lambda x \in T$. Thus we see that T is a subspace of V. $\diamond$

In contrast with the above situation, we note that the union of a collection of subspaces of a vector space V need not in general be a subspace of V :

Example In $\mathbb{R}^2$ the x-axis X and the y-axis Y are subspaces, but their union is not; for example, we have $(1, 0) \in X$ and $(0, 1) \in Y$ but $(1, 0) + (0, 1) = (1, 1) \notin X \cup Y$ so the subset $X \cup Y$ is not closed under addition and therefore cannot be a subspace.

Suppose now that we are given a subset S of a vector space V (with no restrictions, so that S may be empty if we wish). The collection C of all the subspaces of V that contain S is not empty, for clearly V belongs to C. By 5.2, the intersection of all the subspaces in C is also a subspace of V, and clearly this intersection also contains S. This intersection is therefore the smallest subspace of V that contains S (and is, of course, S itself whenever S is a subspace). We shall denote this subspace by $\langle S \rangle$.

Example In $\mathbb{R}^2$ let $S = \{(x, y)\}$. Then $\langle S \rangle$ is the line joining (x, y) to the origin.

Our immediate objective is to characterize the subspace $\langle S \rangle$ in a useful alternative way. For this purpose, we consider first the case where S is not empty and introduce the following notion.

Definition Let V be a vector space over a field F and let S be a non-empty subset of V. Then we say that $v \in V$ is a *linear combination of elements of S* if there exist $x_1, \ldots, x_n \in S$ and $\lambda_1, \ldots, \lambda_n \in F$ such that

$$v = \lambda_1 x_1 + \cdots + \lambda_n x_n = \sum_{i=1}^{n} \lambda_i x_i.$$

It is clear that if $v = \sum_{i=1}^{n} \lambda_i x_i$ and $w = \sum_{j=1}^{m} \mu_j x_j$ are linear combinations of elements of S then so is $v + w$; moreover, so is λv for every $\lambda \in F$. Thus the set of linear combinations of elements of S is a subspace of V. We call this the *subspace spanned by S* and denote it by $\operatorname{Span} S$.

5.3 Theorem $\langle S \rangle = \operatorname{Span} S$.

Proof For every $x \in S$ we have $x = 1_F x \in \operatorname{Span} S$ and so it follows that $S \subseteq \operatorname{Span} S$. Since, by definition, $\langle S \rangle$ is the smallest subspace that contains S, it follows from the fact that $\operatorname{Span} S$ is a subspace that $\langle S \rangle \subseteq \operatorname{Span} S$. To establish the reverse inclusion, let $x_1, \ldots, x_n \in S$ and $\lambda_1, \ldots, \lambda_n \in F$. Then if W is any subspace of V that contains S we clearly have $x_1, \ldots, x_n \in W$ and so $\lambda_1 x_1 + \cdots + \lambda_n x_n \in W$. Consequently we see that $\operatorname{Span} S \subseteq W$. Taking in particular W to be $\langle S \rangle$, we obtain the result. $\Diamond$

An important special case of the above arises when $\operatorname{Span} S$ is the whole of V. In this case we often say that S is a *spanning set* for V.

Example Consider the subset $S = \{(1, 0), (0, 1)\}$ of the cartesian plane $\mathbb{R}^2$. For every $(x, y) \in \mathbb{R}^2$ we have

$$(x, y) = (x, 0) + (0, y) = x(1, 0) + y(0, 1),$$

so that every element of $\mathbb{R}^2$ is a linear combination of elements of S. Thus S spans $\mathbb{R}^2$.

Example More generally, if $e_i = (0, \ldots, 0, 1, 0, \ldots, 0)$ is an n-tuple with the 1 in the i-th position then we have

$$(x_1, \ldots, x_n) = x_1 e_1 + \cdots + x_n e_n,$$

and so $\{e_1, \ldots, e_n\}$ spans $\mathbb{R}^n$.

Example In $\mathbb{R}^3$ we have

$$\mathrm{Span}\{(1,0,0)\} = \{\lambda(1,0,0) \; ; \; \lambda \in \mathbb{R}\} = \{(\lambda,0,0) \; ; \; \lambda \in \mathbb{R}\}.$$

In other words, the subspace of $\mathbb{R}^3$ that is spanned by $\{(1,0,0)\}$ is the x-axis.

Example In $\mathbb{R}^3$ we have

$$\begin{aligned}
\mathrm{Span}\{(1,0,0),(0,0,1)\} &= \{x(1,0,0) + z(0,0,1) \; ; \; x,z \in \mathbb{R}\} \\
&= \{(x,0,z) \; ; \; x,z \in \mathbb{R}\}.
\end{aligned}$$

In other words, the subspace of $\mathbb{R}^3$ that is spanned by the subset $\{(1,0,0),(0,0,1)\}$ is the 'x,z-plane'.

We now formalise, for an arbitrary vector space, another notion that we have seen before when dealing with matrices.

Definition A non-empty subset S of a vector space V over a field F is said to be *linearly independent* if the only way of expressing 0_V as a linear combination of elements of S is the trivial way (in which all the scalars are 0_F); equivalently, if $x_1,\ldots,x_n \in S$ and $\lambda_1,\ldots,\lambda_n \in F$ then

$$\lambda_1 x_1 + \cdots + \lambda_n x_n = 0_V \implies \lambda_1 = \cdots = \lambda_n = 0_F.$$

Example $\{(1,0),(0,1)\}$ is a linearly independent subset of $\mathbb{R}^2$; for if $\lambda(1,0) + \mu(0,1) = (0,0)$ then $(\lambda,\mu) = (0,0)$ and hence $\lambda = \mu = 0$.

Example More generally, if $e_i = (0,\ldots,0,1,0,\ldots,0)$ with the 1 in the i-th position then $\{e_1,\ldots,e_n\}$ is a linearly independent subset of $\mathbb{R}^n$.

Example Every singleton subset $\{x\}$ of V with $x \neq 0_V$ is linearly independent. This is immediate from 5.1(3).

The following result is proved exactly as in 3.7 :

5.4 Theorem *No linearly independent subset of a vector space V can contain 0_V.* $\diamond$

A subset that is not linearly independent is said to be *linearly dependent*. Note that by the last example above every such subset other than $\{0_V\}$ must contain at least two elements. Linearly dependent subsets can be characterized in the following useful way, the proof of which is exactly as in 3.8 :

5.5 Theorem *Let V be a vector space over a field F. If S is a subset of V containing at least two elements then the following statements are equivalent :*

(1) *S is linearly dependent;*

(2) *at least one element of S can be expressed as a linear combination of the other elements of S.* $\diamond$

Example $\{(1,1,0),(2,5,3),(0,1,1)\}$ is linearly dependent in $\mathbb{R}^3$; for we have that $(2,5,3) = 2(1,1,0) + 3(0,1,1)$.

Example If x, y are elements of a vector space V then $\{x, y\}$ is a linearly dependent subset of V if and only if either $y = \lambda x$ or $x = \lambda y$, for some non-zero λ. This is immediate from 5.5.

We now combine the notions of a linearly independent set and a spanning set to obtain the following important concept.

Definition By a *basis* of a vector space V we mean a linearly independent subset of V that spans V.

Example $\{(1,0),(0,1)\}$ is a basis for the cartesian plane $\mathbb{R}^2$. Likewise $\{(1,0,0),(0,1,0),(0,0,1)\}$ is a basis for $\mathbb{R}^3$, and more generally $\{e_1,\ldots,e_n\}$ is a basis for $\mathbb{R}^n$. These bases are called the *natural* (or *canonical*) bases.

Example $\{(1,1),(1,-1)\}$ is a basis for $\mathbb{R}^2$. In fact, for every $(x, y) \in \mathbb{R}^2$ we have $(x, y) = \lambda(1,1) + \mu(1,-1)$ where $\lambda = \frac{1}{2}(x + y)$ and $\mu = \frac{1}{2}(x-y)$, so $\{(1,1),(1,-1)\}$ spans $\mathbb{R}^2$; and if $\alpha(1,1) + \beta(1,-1) = (0,0)$ then $\alpha + \beta = 0$ and $\alpha - \beta = 0$ whence $\alpha = \beta = 0$, so $\{(1,1),(1,-1)\}$ is also linearly independent.

A fundamental characterization of bases is the following.

5.6 Theorem *A non-empty subset S of a vector space V is a basis if and only if every element of V can be expressed in a unique way as a linear combination of elements of S.*

Proof $\Rightarrow$: Suppose first that S is a basis of V. Then we have $\operatorname{Span} S = V$ and so, by 5.3, every $x \in V$ is a linear combination of elements of S. Since S is linearly independent, only one such linear combination is possible for each $x \in V$; for clearly $\sum \lambda_i x_i = \sum \mu_i x_i$ gives $\sum (\lambda_i - \mu_i) x_i = 0_V$ so $\lambda_i = \mu_i$ for all i.

$\Leftarrow$: Suppose, conversely, that every element of V can be expressed in a unique way as a linear combination of elements of

S. Then clearly Span S is the whole of V. Moreover, 0_V can be expressed in only one way as a linear combination of elements of S, and this must be the one in which all the scalars are 0_F, so S is also linearly independent. Thus S is a basis of V. $\diamond$

Example Let $\mathbb{R}_{n+1}[X]$ be the vector space of real polynomials of degree at most n. Then $\{1, X, X^2, \ldots, X^n\}$ is a basis of this vector space. For, every polynomial of degree at most n can be written uniquely in the form

$$a_0 + a_1 X + a_2 X^2 + \cdots + a_n X^n.$$

Example For $i = 1, \ldots, n$ let $a_i = (a_{i1}, a_{i2}, \ldots, a_{in})$. Then the set $\{a_1, \ldots, a_n\}$ is a basis of $\mathbb{R}^n$ if and only if the matrix $A = [a_{ij}]_{n \times n}$ is invertible (equivalently, is of rank n). To see this, let $x = (x_1, \ldots, x_n) \in \mathbb{R}^n$ and consider the equation

$$x = \lambda_1 a_1 + \lambda_2 a_2 + \cdots + \lambda_n a_n.$$

By equating corresponding components we see that this is equivalent to the system

$$x_1 = \lambda_1 a_{11} + \lambda_2 a_{21} + \cdots + \lambda_n a_{n1}$$
$$x_2 = \lambda_1 a_{12} + \lambda_2 a_{22} + \cdots + \lambda_n a_{n2}$$
$$\vdots$$
$$x_n = \lambda_1 a_{1n} + \lambda_2 a_{2n} + \cdots + \lambda_n a_{nn}$$

i.e. to the system

$$A^t \begin{bmatrix} \lambda_1 \\ \vdots \\ \lambda_n \end{bmatrix} = \begin{bmatrix} x_1 \\ \vdots \\ x_n \end{bmatrix}$$

where $A = [a_{ij}]_{n \times n}$. From these observations we see that every $x \in \mathbb{R}^n$ can be written uniquely as a linear combination of $a_1, \ldots, a_n$ if and only if the above matrix equation has a unique solution. This is so if and only if A^t is invertible, which is the case if and only if A is invertible (equivalently, if A has maximum rank n).

Example Consider the set of all real sequences $(a_n)_{n \geq 1}$. We can make this into a real vector space in an obvious way, namely by defining addition and multiplication by scalars as follows :

$$(a_n)_{n \geq 1} + (b_n)_{n \geq 1} = (a_n + b_n)_{n \geq 1}, \quad \lambda(a_n)_{n \geq 1} = (\lambda a_n)_{n \geq 1}.$$

Define a sequence to be *finite* if there is some element of the sequence with the property that all subsequent elements in the sequence are 0; i.e. there is an element a_m such that $a_p = 0$ for all $p > m$. Clearly, the set of all finite sequences is a subspace of the space of all sequences. Consider now the (finite) sequences that are represented as follows :

$$e_1 = 1, 0, 0, 0, \ldots$$
$$e_2 = 0, 1, 0, 0, \ldots$$
$$e_3 = 0, 0, 1, 0, \ldots$$
$$\vdots$$
$$e_i = \underbrace{0, 0, 0, 0, \ldots, 0}_{i-1}, 1, 0, 0, \ldots$$
$$\vdots$$

Clearly, $\{e_1, e_2, e_3, \ldots\}$ forms a basis for the vector space of all finite sequences. Note that this basis is infinite.

Our objective now is to prove that if a vector space V has a finite basis B then every basis of V is also finite and has the same number of elements as B. This is a consequence of the following result.

5.7 Theorem *Let V be a vector space that is spanned by the (finite) set $\{v_1, \ldots, v_n\}$. If $I = \{w_1, \ldots, w_m\}$ is a linearly independent subset of V then necessarily $m \leq n$.*

Proof Consider $w_1 \in I$. There exist scalars $\lambda_1, \ldots, \lambda_n$ such that $w_1 = \lambda_1 v_1 + \cdots + \lambda_n v_n$ and at least one of the λ_i is non-zero (otherwise every λ_i is 0_F, whence w_1 is 0_V, and this contradicts 5.4). By a suitable change of indices, we can take $\lambda_1 \neq 0_F$. Then we have

$$v_1 = \lambda_1^{-1} w_1 - \lambda_1^{-1} \lambda_2 v_2 - \cdots - \lambda_1^{-1} \lambda_n v_n,$$

which shows that

$$V = \mathrm{Span}\{v_1, v_2, \ldots, v_n\} \subseteq \mathrm{Span}\{w_1, v_2, \ldots, v_n\}.$$

It follows that $V = \mathrm{Span}\{w_1, v_2, \ldots, v_n\}$. Repeating this argument with v_2, we can show similarly that

$$V = \mathrm{Span}\{w_1, w_2, v_3, \ldots, v_n\}.$$

Continuing in this way, we see that if $p = \min\{m, n\}$ then

$$V = \mathrm{Span}\{w_1, \ldots, w_p, v_{p+1}, \ldots, v_n\}.$$

Now we see that $m > n$ is impossible; for in this case $p = n$ and we would have $V = \mathrm{Span}\{w_1, \ldots, w_n\}$ whence the elements $w_{n+1}, \ldots, w_m$ would be linear combinations of $w_1, \ldots, w_n$ and this would contradict the fact that I is independent. Thus we conclude that necessarily $m \leq n$. $\diamond$

5.8 Corollary *If V has a finite basis B then every basis of V is finite and has the same number of elements as B.*

Proof Suppose that $B^\star$ were an infinite basis of V. Since clearly every subset of a linearly independent set is also linearly independent, every subset of $B^\star$ is linearly independent. There would therefore exist a finite linearly independent subset consisting of more elements than B has; and this is not possible by 5.7. Consequently we see that all bases of V must also be finite.

Suppose now that B has n elements and let $B^\star$ be a basis having $n^\star$ elements. Again by 5.7, we have $n^\star \leq n$. But, inverting the roles of B and $B^\star$, we also have $n \leq n^\star$. Thus $n^\star = n$ and so all bases have the same number of elements. $\diamond$

Because of the above result, we can introduce the following notion.

Definition By a *finite-dimensional* vector space we shall mean a vector space V that has a finite basis. The number of elements in any basis of V is called the *dimension* of V and will be denoted by $\dim V$.

Example $\mathbb{R}^n$ has dimension n.

Example The vector space $\text{Mat}_{m \times n}(\mathbb{R})$ is of dimension mn. In fact, as is readily seen, if E_{ij} is the $m \times n$ matrix that has 1 in the (i,j)-th position and 0 elsewhere then $\{E_{ij} \; ; \; i = 1, \ldots, m \text{ and } j = 1, \ldots, n\}$ is a basis for $\text{Mat}_{m \times n}(\mathbb{R})$.

Example The vector space $\mathbb{R}_{n+1}[X]$ of real polynomials of degree at most n is of dimension $n + 1$. In fact, $\{1, X, X^2, \ldots, X^n\}$ is a basis for this space.

Example The set V of complex matrices of the form

$$\begin{bmatrix} \alpha & \beta \\ \gamma & -\alpha \end{bmatrix}$$

forms a real vector space of dimension 6. In fact the matrix

$$\begin{bmatrix} a + ib & c + id \\ e + if & -a - ib \end{bmatrix}$$

can be written as

$$a\begin{bmatrix} 1 & 0 \\ 0 & -1 \end{bmatrix} + b\begin{bmatrix} i & 0 \\ 0 & -i \end{bmatrix} + c\begin{bmatrix} 0 & 1 \\ 0 & 0 \end{bmatrix} + d\begin{bmatrix} 0 & i \\ 0 & 0 \end{bmatrix} + e\begin{bmatrix} 0 & 0 \\ 1 & 0 \end{bmatrix} + f\begin{bmatrix} 0 & 0 \\ i & 0 \end{bmatrix}$$

and as the six matrices involved in this linear combination belong to V, and are clearly linearly independent over $\mathbb{R}$, they form a basis for the subspace that they span, namely V.

Example The set W of complex matrices of the form

$$\begin{bmatrix} \alpha & \beta \\ -\overline{\beta} & -\alpha \end{bmatrix}$$

is a real vector space of dimension 4. In fact, the matrix

$$\begin{bmatrix} a + ib & c + id \\ -c + id & -a - ib \end{bmatrix}$$

can be written as

$$a\begin{bmatrix} 1 & 0 \\ 0 & -1 \end{bmatrix} + b\begin{bmatrix} i & 0 \\ 0 & -i \end{bmatrix} + c\begin{bmatrix} 0 & 1 \\ -1 & 0 \end{bmatrix} + d\begin{bmatrix} 0 & i \\ i & 0 \end{bmatrix}$$

and as the four matrices involved in this linear combination belong to W and are clearly linearly independent over $\mathbb{R}$ they form a basis for the subspace that they span, namely W.

It is convenient to regard the empty set $\emptyset$ as being linearly independent, the justification for this being that the condition for a set of elements to be linearly independent is satisfied 'vacuously' by $\emptyset$. Now the smallest subspace of V that contains $\emptyset$ is clearly the zero subspace $\{0_V\}$, so we can regard the zero subspace as being spanned by $\emptyset$. These courtesies concerning $\emptyset$ mean that we can usefully regard $\emptyset$ as a basis for the zero subspace, which we can then say has dimension 0.

We shall now establish some important facts concerning bases.

5.9 Theorem *Let V be a finite-dimensional vector space. If G is a finite spanning set for V and if I is a linearly independent subset of V such that $I \subseteq G$ then there is a basis B of V such that $I \subseteq B \subseteq G$.*

Proof If I also spans V then I is a basis and there is nothing to prove. Suppose then that $\operatorname{Span} I \neq V$. Then we must have $I \subset G$ and we note first that there then exists $g_1 \in G \setminus I$ such that $g_1 \notin \operatorname{Span} I$; for otherwise every element of $G \setminus I$ belongs to $\operatorname{Span} I$ whence $V = \operatorname{Span} G \subseteq \operatorname{Span} I$ and we have the contradiction $V = \operatorname{Span} I$. We now observe that $I \cup \{g_1\}$ is linearly independent; for otherwise we would have $g_1 \in \operatorname{Span} I$. Now if $I \cup \{g_1\}$ spans V then it is a basis, in which case no more proof is required since we simply take $B = I \cup \{g_1\}$. If not, then we repeat the above argument to produce an element g_2 in $G \setminus (I \cup \{g_1\})$ with $I \cup \{g_1, g_2\}$ linearly independent. Since G is finite it then follows that, for some m, $B = I \cup \{g_1, \ldots, g_m\}$ is a basis for V with $I \subset B \subseteq G$. $\diamond$

5.10 Corollary *Every linearly independent subset I of a finite-dimensional vector space can be enlarged to form a basis.*

Proof Take $G = I \cup B$ where B is any basis of V. Then by 5.9 there is a basis B^* with $I \subseteq B^* \subseteq I \cup B$. $\diamond$

5.11 Corollary *If V is of dimension n then every linearly independent set consisting of n elements is a basis of V.*

Proof This is immediate from 5.10 and 5.8. $\diamond$

5.12 Corollary *If S is a subset of V then the following statements are equivalent:*

(1) *S is a basis;*

   (2) S is a maximal independent subset (in the sense that if I is an independent subset with $S \subseteq I$ then $S = I$);

   (3) S is a minimal spanning set (in the sense that if G spans V and $G \subseteq S$ then $G = S$).

Proof (1) $\Rightarrow$ (2) : If I is independent with $S \subseteq I$ then by 5.10 there is a basis B with $I \subseteq B$. Since S is a basis, and since all bases have the same number of elements, we deduce that $S = B = I$.

   (2) $\Rightarrow$ (1) : By 5.10 there is a basis B with $S \subseteq B$. But B is also independent, so by (2) we have $S = B$ and so S is a basis.

   (1) $\Rightarrow$ (3) : If G spans V then (recalling that $\emptyset$ is independent) there is a basis B with $\emptyset \subseteq B \subseteq G$. If $G \subseteq S$ then $B \subseteq S$ and both are bases, and therefore have the same number of elements. We deduce that $B = G = S$.

   (3) $\Rightarrow$ (1) : There is a basis B with $\emptyset \subseteq B \subseteq S$. But B also spans V so, by (3), $B = S$ and S is a basis. $\diamond$

5.13 Corollary If V is of dimension n then every subset containing more than n elements is linearly dependent; and no subset containing fewer than n elements can span V.

Proof This is immediate from 5.12. $\diamond$

   We now enquire about bases for subspaces of a given finite-dimensional vector space.

5.14 Theorem Let V be a finite-dimensional vector space. If W is a subspace of V then W is also of finite dimension, and $\dim W \leq \dim V$. Moreover, we have $\dim W = \dim V$ if and only if $W = V$.

Proof Suppose that $\dim W = n$. For every subspace W of V let $N(W)$ be the set of non-negative integers p such that W has linearly independent subsets consisting of p elements. By 5.7 we clearly have $N(W) \subseteq \{0, 1, \ldots, n\}$ so $N(W)$ has a greatest element, m say. Suppose that J is a linearly independent subset of W having m elements. Then Span $J \subseteq W$, and we shall show that in fact Span $J = W$. For this purpose, suppose that Span $J \neq W$. Then there exists $t \in W$ such that $t \notin$ Span J. Since t is not a linear combination of elements of J, we see that $J \cup \{t\}$ is an independent subset of W consisting of $m + 1$ elements. This contradicts the maximality of m; and from this contradiction we deduce that $\text{Span} \, J = W$. Now by hypothesis J is a linearly independent subset of W, so we have that J is a basis of W. Thus W is of finite dimension with $\dim W = m \leq n = \dim V$.

Finally, if $m = n$ then J is an independent subset consisting of n elements whence, by 5.11, J is a basis of V. Consequently we have $W = \text{Span} \, J = V$. $\diamond$

Example Consider the real vector space $\mathbb{R}^2$. This is of dimension 2 and so if W is any subspace of $\mathbb{R}^2$ then by 5.14 the dimension of W must be 0, 1, or 2. If $\dim W = 0$ then we have $W = \{(0, 0)\}$, and if $\dim W = 2$ we have $W = \mathbb{R}^2$. In the case where $\dim W = 1$ we see that W has a basis consisting of a single element (x, y) so that

$$W = \{\lambda(x, y) \; ; \; \lambda \in \mathbb{R}\} = \{(\lambda x, \lambda y) \; ; \; \lambda \in \mathbb{R}\},$$

which is none other than the line passing through the origin $(0, 0)$ and the point (x, y).

Example Arguing in a similar way, we can show that the subspaces of $\mathbb{R}^3$ are $\{(0, 0, 0)\}$, any line through the origin, any plane through the origin, and $\mathbb{R}^3$ itself; these correspond to the dimensions $0, 1, 2, 3$ respectively.

CHAPTER SIX

Linear mappings

In the study of any algebraic structure there are two concepts that are of paramount importance. The first is that of a *substructure* (i.e. a subset with the same type of structure), and the second is that of a *morphism* (i.e. a mapping from one structure to another that is 'structure-preserving'). So far we have encountered the notion of a substructure for vector spaces; this we called a *subspace*. In this Chapter we shall consider the notion of a morphism between vector spaces, that is a mapping f from one vector space to another that is 'structure-preserving' in the following sense.

Definition If V and W are vector spaces over the same field F then by a *linear mapping* (or *linear transformation*) from V to W we shall mean a mapping $f : V \to W$ such that

(1) $(\forall x, y \in V)\quad f(x+y) = f(x) + f(y)$;
(2) $(\forall x \in V)(\forall \lambda \in F)\quad f(\lambda x) = \lambda f(x)$.

Note that in this definition we have introduced a new symbol '$\forall$'. This is to be read 'for all' or 'for every'.

Example The mapping $f : \mathbb{R}^2 \to \mathbb{R}^3$ given by

$$f(x,y) = (x+y, x-y, y)$$

is linear, for it is readily verified that (1) and (2) above hold.

Example For $i = 1, \ldots, n$ let $\mathrm{pr}_i : \mathbb{R}^n \to \mathbb{R}$ be the mapping described by $\mathrm{pr}_i(x_1, \ldots, x_n) = x_i$. In other words, pr_i is the mapping that picks out the i-th coordinate. It is readily seen that pr_i is a linear mapping. We call it the *i-th projection* of $\mathbb{R}^n$ onto $\mathbb{R}$.

Example Let $\mathbb{R}_{n+1}[X]$ be the vector space of all real polynomials of degree at most n. Then the differentiation mapping $D : \mathbb{R}_{n+1}[X] \to \mathbb{R}_{n+1}[X]$ described by

$$D(a_0 + a_1 X + \cdots + a_n X^n) = a_1 + 2a_2 X + \cdots + n a_n X^{n-1}$$

is linear, for if $p(X), q(X)$ are such polynomials then we know that $D(p(X) + q(X)) = Dp(X) + Dq(X)$ and $D(\lambda p(X)) = \lambda Dp(X)$.

The following result contains two important properties of linear mappings that will be used constantly in what follows.

6.1 Theorem *If the mapping* $f : V \to W$ *is linear then*

(1) $f(0_V) = 0_W$;
(2) $(\forall x \in V) \quad f(-x) = -f(x)$.

Proof (1) $f(0_V) = f(0_F 0_V) = 0_F f(0_V) = 0_W$.

(2) Using (1) we have, for every $x \in V$, $f(x) + f(-x) = f[x + (-x)] = f(0_V) = 0_W$ from which the result follows. $\diamondsuit$

We shall now consider some important subsets that are associated with linear mappings. For this purpose we introduce the following notation. If $f : V \to W$ is linear then for every subset X of V we define $f^{\to}(X)$ to be the subset of W given by

$$f^{\to}(X) = \{f(x) \; ; \; x \in X\},$$

and for every subset Y of W we define $f^{\leftarrow}(Y)$ to be the subset of V given by

$$f^{\leftarrow}(Y) = \{x \in V \; ; \; f(x) \in Y\}.$$

The reader should be warned that this is not 'standard' notation, in the sense that most authors write $f(X)$ for $f^{\to}(X)$, and $f^{-1}(Y)$ for $f^{\leftarrow}(Y)$. We introduce this notation in order to reserve the notation f^{-1} as the standard notation for the inverse of a bijection. One advantage that this non-standard notation has to offer is that it gives a visually appealing reminder, namely that $f^{\to}$ sends subsets of V to subsets of W, and $f^{\leftarrow}$ lifts back subsets of W to subsets of V.

It is clear that both $f^{\to}$ and $f^{\leftarrow}$ are *inclusion-preserving* in the sense that if $X_1 \subseteq X_2$ then $f^{\to}(X_1) \subseteq f^{\to}(X_2)$, and if $Y_1 \subseteq Y_2$ then $f^{\leftarrow}(Y_1) \subseteq f^{\leftarrow}(Y_2)$. We now show that in fact each of these mappings carries subspaces to subspaces.

6.2 Theorem *Let $f : V \to W$ be linear. If X is a subspace of V then $f^{\to}(X)$ is a subspace of W ; and if Y is a subspace of W then $f^{\leftarrow}(Y)$ is a subspace of V.*

Proof If X is a subspace of V then $0_V \in X$ so $0_W = f(0_V) \in f^{\to}(X)$ and hence $f^{\to}(X) \neq \emptyset$. If now $x, y \in f^{\to}(X)$ then $x = f(a)$ and $y = f(b)$ for some $a, b \in X$ whence $x + y = f(a) + f(b) = f(a + b) \in f^{\to}(X)$; and $\lambda x = \lambda f(a) = f(\lambda a) \in f^{\to}(X)$. Thus $f^{\to}(X)$ is a subspace of W.

Suppose now that Y is a subspace of W. Then $f(0_V) = 0_W \in Y$ so $0_V \in f^{\leftarrow}(Y)$ and hence $f^{\leftarrow}(Y) \neq \emptyset$. If now $x, y \in f^{\leftarrow}(Y)$ then $f(x), f(y) \in Y$ whence $f(x + y) = f(x) + f(y) \in Y$ and so $x + y \in f^{\leftarrow}(Y)$; and $f(\lambda x) = \lambda f(x) \in Y$ so $\lambda x \in f^{\leftarrow}(Y)$. Thus $f^{\leftarrow}(Y)$ is a subspace of V. $\Diamond$

Given a linear map $f : V \to W$, we sometimes call $f^{\to}(X)$ the *direct image* of X under f, and $f^{\leftarrow}(Y)$ the *inverse image* of Y under f. Of particular importance are the biggest direct image and the smallest inverse image. The former is $f^{\to}(V)$; it is called the *image* (or *range*) of f and is written Im f. The latter is $f^{\leftarrow}(\{0_W\})$; it is called the *kernel* (or *null-space*) of f and is written Ker f. Pictorially, these sets are depicted as follows :

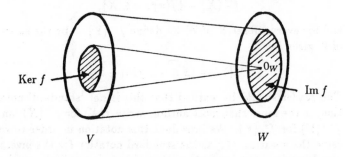

Ker f — 0_W — Im f

V　　　　W

Example The image of the i-th projection $\mathrm{pr}_i : \mathbb{R}^n \to \mathbb{R}$ is the whole of $\mathbb{R}$, and the kernel of this mapping is the set of n-tuples whose i-th component is 0.

Example Consider the differentiation map $D : \mathbb{R}_{n+1}[X] \to \mathbb{R}_{n+1}[X]$. Its image is the set of all real polynomials of degree at most $n - 1$; i.e, it is $\mathbb{R}_n[X]$. The kernel of D is the set of polynomials whose derivative is zero, i.e. the set of constant polynomials, i.e. $\mathbb{R}$.

Example If A is a given real $n \times n$ matrix, consider the mapping

$$f_A : \text{Mat}_{n \times 1}(\mathbb{R}) \to \text{Mat}_{n \times 1}(\mathbb{R})$$

described by $f_A(\mathbf{x}) = A\mathbf{x}$. This mapping is linear since clearly $A(\mathbf{x} + \mathbf{y}) = A\mathbf{x} + A\mathbf{y}$ and $A(\lambda \mathbf{x}) = \lambda A\mathbf{x}$. The image of f_A consists of all column matrices $\mathbf{y} = [y_1 \ \ldots \ y_n]^t$ for which there exists a column matrix $\mathbf{x} = [x_1 \ \ldots \ x_n]^t$ such that $A\mathbf{x} = \mathbf{y}$; i.e. the set of all $\mathbf{y}$ such that there exist $x_1, \ldots, x_n$ with

$$\mathbf{y} = x_1 \mathbf{a}_1 + \cdots + x_n \mathbf{a}_n,$$

where $\mathbf{a}_i$ denotes the i-th column of A. In other words, $\text{Im} f_A$ is the subspace of $\text{Mat}_{n \times 1}(\mathbb{R})$ that is spanned by the columns of A. As for the kernel of f_A, this is the subspace of $\text{Mat}_{n \times 1}(\mathbb{R})$ consisting of the column matrices $\mathbf{x}$ such that $A\mathbf{x} = \mathbf{0}$; i.e. the *solution space* of the equation $f_A(\mathbf{x}) = \mathbf{0}$.

Example Consider the subspace of $\text{Map}(\mathbb{R}, \mathbb{R})$ that is given by $V = \text{Span}\{\sin, \cos\}$. Let $L : V \to \mathbb{R}$ be given by

$$L(f) = \int_0^\pi f(t)\, dt.$$

By basic properties of integrals, L is linear. Now every $f \in V$ is of the form $a \sin t + b \cos t$, and such an f belongs to $\text{Ker} L$ if and only if

$$\int_0^\pi (a \sin t + b \cos t)\, dt = 0.$$

But this is the case if and only if $a = 0$, so we deduce that $\text{Ker} L = \text{Span}\{\cos\}$.

6.3 Theorem *A linear mapping $f : V \to W$ is surjective if and only if $\text{Im} f = W$; and is injective if and only if $\text{Ker} f = \{0_V\}$.*

Proof To say that f is surjective is equivalent to saying that every $y \in W$ is of the form $f(x)$ for some $x \in V$; so f is surjective if and only if $W = \text{Im} f$.

Suppose now that f is injective, i.e. that $f(x) = f(y)$ implies $x = y$. If $x \in \text{Ker} f$ then we have $f(x) = 0_W = f(0_V)$ whence

$x = 0_V$ and consequently $\operatorname{Ker} f = \{0_V\}$. Conversely, if $\operatorname{Ker} f = \{0_V\}$ and $f(x) = f(y)$ then $f(x - y) = f[x + (-y)] = f(x) + f(-y) = f(x) - f(y) = 0_W$ so that $x - y \in \operatorname{Ker} f = \{0_V\}$ and hence $x = y$, i.e. f is injective. $\Diamond$

Henceforth, we shall write 0_F and 0_V as simply 0.

We now show that, in the case of finite-dimensional vector spaces, there is an important connection between the dimensions of the subspaces $\operatorname{Im} f$ and $\operatorname{Ker} f$.

6.4 Theorem [Dimension theorem] *Let V and W be vector spaces of finite dimension over a field F. If $f : V \to W$ is linear then*

$$\dim V = \dim \operatorname{Im} f + \dim \operatorname{Ker} f.$$

Proof Let $\{w_1, \ldots, w_m\}$ be a basis for the subspace $\operatorname{Im} f$ and let $\{v_1, \ldots, v_n\}$ be a basis for the subspace $\operatorname{Ker} f$. Since each $w_i \in \operatorname{Im} f$ we can choose $v_1^\star, \ldots, v_m^\star \in V$ such that $w_i = f(v_i^\star)$ for $i = 1, \ldots, m$. We shall show that $\{v_1^\star, \ldots, v_m^\star, v_1, \ldots, v_n\}$ is a basis for V, whence the result follows.

Suppose then that $x \in V$. Since $f(x) \in \operatorname{Im} f$ there exist scalars $\lambda_1, \ldots, \lambda_m$ such that

$$f(x) = \sum_{i=1}^{m} \lambda_i w_i = \sum_{i=1}^{m} \lambda_i f(v_i^\star) = \sum_{i=1}^{m} f(\lambda_i v_i^\star) = f\left(\sum_{i=1}^{m} \lambda_i v_i^\star\right).$$

It follows that $x - \sum_{i=1}^{m} \lambda_i v_i^\star \in \operatorname{Ker} f$ and so there exist scalars $\mu_1, \ldots, \mu_n$ such that

$$x - \sum_{i=1}^{m} \lambda_i v_i^\star = \sum_{j=1}^{n} \mu_j v_j.$$

Thus every $x \in V$ can be expressed as a linear combination of $v_1^\star, \ldots, v_m^\star, v_1, \ldots, v_n$, and so $V = \operatorname{Span}\{v_1^\star, \ldots, v_m^\star, v_1, \ldots, v_n\}$. Suppose now that

$$(\star) \qquad \sum_{i=1}^{m} \lambda_i v_i^\star + \sum_{j=1}^{n} \mu_j v_j = 0.$$

Then we have

$$\sum_{i=1}^{m} \lambda_i v_i^\star = -\sum_{j=1}^{n} \mu_j v_j \in \operatorname{Ker} f$$

and consequently

$$\sum_{i=1}^{m} \lambda_i w_i = \sum_{i=1}^{m} \lambda_i f(v_i^\star) = f\left(\sum_{i=1}^{m} \lambda_i v_i^\star\right) = 0$$

whence $\lambda_1 = \cdots = \lambda_m = 0$ since $\{w_1, \ldots, w_m\}$ is a basis for
Im f. It now follows from $(\star)$ that $\sum_{j=1}^{n} \mu_j v_j = 0$ whence $\mu_1 =$
$\cdots = \mu_n = 0$ since $\{v_1, \ldots, v_n\}$ is a basis for Ker f. Thus we
see that the spanning set $\{v_1^\star, \ldots, v_m^\star, v_1, \ldots, v_n\}$ is also linearly
independent and is therefore a basis for V. $\diamond$

Example Consider the projection $\mathrm{pr}_1 : \mathbb{R}^3 \to \mathbb{R}$ given by
$\mathrm{pr}_1(x, y, z) = x$. Clearly, Im $\mathrm{pr}_1 = \mathbb{R}$ which is of dimension
1 since $\{1\}$ is a basis of the real vector space $\mathbb{R}$; and Ker pr_1
is the y, z-plane which is of dimension 2. Then dim Im $\mathrm{pr}_1 +$
dim Ker $\mathrm{pr}_1 = 3$ which is the dimension of $\mathbb{R}^3$.

If f is a linear mapping then dim Im f is called the *rank* of f,
and dim Ker f is called the *nullity* of f. With this terminology,
the dimension theorem can be stated in the form :

rank + nullity = dimension of departure space.

As an application of the dimension theorem, we establish another result that is somewhat surprising.

6.5 Theorem *Let V and W be vector spaces each of dimension
n over a field F. If $f : V \to W$ is linear then the following
statements are equivalent :*

(1) *f is injective;*
(2) *f is surjective;*
(3) *f is bijective;*
(4) *f carries bases to bases, in the sense that if $\{v_1, \ldots, v_n\}$ is
    a basis of V then $\{f(v_1), \ldots, f(v_n)\}$ is a basis of W.*

Proof (1) $\Rightarrow$ (3) : Suppose that f is injective. Then Ker $f =$
$\{0\}$ and so dim Ker $f = 0$. By 6.4 it follows that dim $W =$
dim $V =$ dim Im f. It now follows by 5.14 that Im $f = W$ and
so f is also surjective, hence is bijective.

(2) $\Rightarrow$ (3) : Suppose that f is surjective. Then Im $f = W$ and
so dim Im $f =$ dim $W =$ dim $V =$ dim Im $f +$ dim Ker f whence

dim Ker $f = 0$ so that Ker $f = \{0\}$ and f is also injective, hence is bijective.

(3) $\Rightarrow$ (1) and (3) $\Rightarrow$ (2) are clear.

(1) $\Rightarrow$ (4) : Suppose that f is injective. If $\{v_1, \ldots, v_n\}$ is a basis of V then the elements $f(v_1), \ldots, f(v_n)$ are distinct. If now $\sum_{i=1}^{n} \lambda_i f(v_i) = 0$ then $f\left(\sum_{i=1}^{n} \lambda_i v_i\right) = 0$ and so, since Ker $f = \{0\}$, we have $\sum_{i=1}^{n} \lambda_i v_i = 0$ and hence $\lambda_1 = \cdots = \lambda_n = 0$. Thus $\{f(v_1), \ldots, f(v_n)\}$ is linearly independent. That it is a basis of W now follows by 5.11.

(4) $\Rightarrow$ (2) : Since every linear combination of $f(v_1), \ldots, f(v_n)$ belongs to Im f it is clear from (4) that Im $f = W$ so that f is surjective. $\diamond$

Definition A bijective linear mapping is called a *linear isomorphism*, or simply an *isomorphism*. We say that vector spaces V, W are *isomorphic*, and write $V \simeq W$, if there is an isomorphism $f : V \to W$.

Example Let $A = \{(x, y, 0) \; ; \; x, y \in \mathbb{R}\}$ be the x, y-plane in $\mathbb{R}^3$, and let $B = \{(x, 0, z) \; ; \; x, z \in \mathbb{R}\}$ be the x, z-plane. Consider the mapping $f : A \to B$ described by $f(x, y, 0) = (x, 0, y)$. It is readily seen that f is linear and bijective. Thus f is an isomorphism and so $A \simeq B$.

This example is a particular case of the following general situation.

6.6 Theorem *Let V be a vector space of dimension $n \geq 1$ over a field F. Then V is isomorphic to the vector space F^n.*

Proof Let $\{v_1, \ldots, v_n\}$ be a basis of V. Consider the mapping $f : V \to F^n$ given by the prescription

$$f\left(\sum_{i=1}^{n} \lambda_i v_i\right) = (\lambda_1, \ldots, \lambda_n).$$

Since for every $x \in V$ there are unique scalars $\lambda_1, \ldots, \lambda_n$ such that $x = \sum_{i=1}^{n} \lambda_i v_i$, it is clear that f is a bijection. It is also linear. Hence it is an isomorphism. $\diamond$

6.7 Corollary *If* V, W *are vector spaces each of dimension* n *over a field* F *then* $V \simeq W$.

Proof There are isomorphisms $f_V : V \to F^n$ and $f_W : W \to F^n$. Since the inverse of an isomorphism is clearly also an isomorphism, so then is the composite $f_W^{-1} \circ f_V : V \to W$. $\diamond$

Our next objective is to prove that a linear mapping enjoys the property that it is completely determined by its action on a basis. This is a consequence of the following result.

6.8 Theorem *Let* V *and* W *be vector spaces over a field* F. *If* $\{v_1, \ldots, v_n\}$ *is a basis of* V *and if* $w_1, \ldots, w_n$ *are elements of* W *(not necessarily distinct) then there is a unique linear mapping* $f : V \to W$ *such that*

$$(i = 1, \ldots, n) \qquad f(v_i) = w_i.$$

Proof Since every element of V can be expressed uniquely in the form $\sum_{i=1}^{n} \lambda_i v_i$, we can define a mapping $f : V \to W$ by the prescription

$$f\left(\sum_{i=1}^{n} \lambda_i v_i\right) = \sum_{i=1}^{n} \lambda_i w_i,$$

i.e. taking x as a linear combination of the basis elements, define $f(x)$ to be the same linear combination of the elements $w_1, \ldots, w_n$. It is readily verified that f is linear. Moreover, for every i,

$$f(v_i) = f\left(\sum_{j=1}^{n} \delta_{ij} v_j\right) = \sum_{j=1}^{n} \delta_{ij} w_j = w_i.$$

To establish the uniqueness of f, suppose that $g : V \to W$ is linear and is such that $g(v_i) = w_i$ for every i. Given $x \in V$, say $x = \sum_{i=1}^{n} \lambda_i v_i$, we have

$$g(x) = \sum_{i=1}^{n} g(\lambda_i v_i) = \sum_{i=1}^{n} \lambda_i g(v_i) = \sum_{i=1}^{n} \lambda_i w_i = f(x)$$

whence $g = f$. $\diamond$

6.9 Corollary *A linear mapping is completely determined by its action on a basis.* $\diamond$

6.10 Corollary *Two linear mappings* $f, g : V \to W$ *are equal if and only if they agree on a basis of* V.

Proof If $f(v_i) = g(v_i)$ for every basis element v_i then by the uniqueness in 6.8 we deduce that $f = g$. $\Diamond$

Example Consider the basis $\{(1,1,0),(1,0,1),(0,1,1)\}$ of $\mathbb{R}^3$. Given that

$$f(1,1,0) = (1,2), \quad f(1,0,1) = (0,0), \quad f(0,1,1) = (2,1),$$

we can determine completely the linear mapping $f : \mathbb{R}^3 \to \mathbb{R}^2$. In fact,

$$(1,0,0) = \tfrac{1}{2}(1,1,0) + \tfrac{1}{2}(1,0,1) - \tfrac{1}{2}(0,1,1)$$

and so we have

$$
\begin{aligned}
f(1,0,0) &= \tfrac{1}{2}f(1,1,0) + \tfrac{1}{2}f(1,0,1) - \tfrac{1}{2}f(0,1,1) \\
&= \tfrac{1}{2}(1,2) + \tfrac{1}{2}(0,0) - \tfrac{1}{2}(2,1) \\
&= (-\tfrac{1}{2}, \tfrac{1}{2}).
\end{aligned}
$$

Likewise,

$$
\begin{aligned}
(0,1,0) &= \tfrac{1}{2}(1,1,0) - \tfrac{1}{2}(0,1,0) + \tfrac{1}{2}(0,1,1), \\
(0,0,1) &= -\tfrac{1}{2}(1,1,0) + \tfrac{1}{2}(1,0,1) + \tfrac{1}{2}(0,1,1)
\end{aligned}
$$

give

$$
\begin{aligned}
f(0,1,0) &= \tfrac{1}{2}(1,2) + \tfrac{1}{2}(2,1) = (\tfrac{3}{2}, \tfrac{3}{2}), \\
f(0,0,1) &= -\tfrac{1}{2}(1,2) + \tfrac{1}{2}(2,1) = (\tfrac{1}{2}, -\tfrac{1}{2}).
\end{aligned}
$$

Consequently, f is given by

$$
\begin{aligned}
f(x,y,z) &= f[x(1,0,0) + y(0,1,0) + z(0,0,1)] \\
&= xf(1,0,0) + yf(0,1,0) + zf(0,0,1) \\
&= x(-\tfrac{1}{2}, \tfrac{1}{2}) + y(\tfrac{3}{2}, \tfrac{3}{2}) + z(\tfrac{1}{2}, -\tfrac{1}{2}) \\
&= \left(\tfrac{1}{2}(-x + 3y + z), \tfrac{1}{2}(x + 3y - z)\right).
\end{aligned}
$$

Alternatively, we could have first expressed (x,y,z) as a linear combination of the given bases elements by solving an appropriate system of equations, then used the given data.

Finally, let us note that 6.5 is not true for vector spaces of infinite dimension :

Example Let V be the infinite-dimensional vector space of finite sequences of real numbers (recall the Example preceding 5.7). By 6.9 we can define a linear mapping $f : V \to V$ by specifying $f(e_i)$ for the basis elements $e_1, e_2, e_3, \ldots$. Consider then the definition

$$f(e_i) = \begin{cases} 0 & \text{if } i \text{ is odd;} \\ e_{\frac{1}{2}i} & \text{if } i \text{ is even.} \end{cases}$$

Since, for example, $f(e_1) = 0 = f(e_3)$ with $e_1 \neq e_3$ we see that f is not injective. However, given any basis element e_n we have $e_n = f(e_{2n}) \in \text{Im } f$, so the subspace spanned by these elements (namely V) is contained in $\text{Im } f$. Hence $\text{Im } f = V$ and so f is surjective. Also, if we define $g : V \to V$ by $g(e_i) = e_{2i}$ then we obtain an injective linear mapping that is not surjective.

CHAPTER SEVEN

The matrix connection

We shall now show how linear mappings on finite-dimensional vector spaces are related to matrices. For this purpose, we require the following notion.

Definition Let V be a finite-dimensional vector space over a field F. By an *ordered basis* of V we shall mean a finite sequence $(a_i)_{1 \leq i \leq n}$ of elements of V such that $\{a_1, \ldots, a_n\}$ is a basis of V.

Note that every basis consisting of n elements gives rise to $n!$ distinct ordered bases, for there are $n!$ permutations on a set of n elements.

In what follows we shall write an ordered basis $(a_i)_{1 \leq i \leq n}$ as simply $(a_i)_n$ for convenience.

Suppose now that V, W are vector spaces of dimensions m, n respectively over a field F. Let $(a_i)_m, (b_i)_n$ be given ordered bases of V, W and let $f : V \rightarrow W$ be linear. We know by 6.9 that f is completely determined by its action on the basis $(a_i)_m$, i.e. by the mn scalars x_{ij} such that

$$f(a_1) = x_{11}b_1 + x_{12}b_2 + \ldots + x_{1n}b_n$$
$$f(a_2) = x_{21}b_1 + x_{22}b_2 + \ldots + x_{2n}b_n$$
$$\vdots$$
$$f(a_m) = x_{m1}b_1 + x_{m2}b_2 + \ldots + x_{mn}b_n.$$

Thus f is determined by the $m \times n$ matrix $X = [x_{ij}]$. For technical reasons that will be explained later, we call the *transpose* of this matrix X the *matrix of f relative to the fixed ordered* *bases* $(a_i)_m, (b_i)_n$ and, when it is obvious what these bases are, we denote it simply by Mat f. The reader should take care to note that it is thus an $n \times m$ matrix that represents a linear map from an m-dimensional space to an n-dimensional space.

Example The mapping $f : \mathbb{R}^3 \to \mathbb{R}^2$ given by

$$f(x, y, z) = (2x - 3y + z, 3x - 2y)$$

is linear. Now the action of f on the standard basis of $\mathbb{R}^3$ is given by

$$\begin{aligned}
f(1, 0, 0) &= & (2, 3) &= & 2(1, 0) + 3(0, 1) \\
f(0, 1, 0) &= & (-3, -2) &= & -3(1, 0) - 2(0, 1) \\
f(0, 0, 1) &= & (1, 0) &= & 1(1, 0) + 0(0, 1)
\end{aligned}$$

and so we see that the matrix of f relative to the standard ordered bases of $\mathbb{R}^3$ and $\mathbb{R}^2$ is the 2×3 matrix

$$\begin{bmatrix} 2 & -3 & 1 \\ 3 & -2 & 0 \end{bmatrix}.$$

Example Let $\mathbb{R}_{n+1}[X]$ be the vector space of polynomials of degree at most n with real coefficients. This vector space has the natural ordered basis $\{1, X, X^2, \ldots, X^n\}$. The differentiation map D is linear, and

$$\begin{aligned}
D1 &= 0 \cdot 1 + 0 \cdot X + \cdots + 0 \cdot X^{n-1} + 0 \cdot X^n \\
DX &= 1 \cdot 1 + 0 \cdot X + \cdots + 0 \cdot X^{n-1} + 0 \cdot X^n \\
DX^2 &= 0 \cdot 1 + 2 \cdot X + \cdots + 0 \cdot X^{n-1} + 0 \cdot X^n \\
&\vdots \\
DX^n &= 0 \cdot 1 + 0 \cdot X + \cdots + n \cdot X^{n-1} + 0 \cdot X^n
\end{aligned}$$

so the matrix of D relative to the natural ordered basis is the $(n + 1) \times (n + 1)$ matrix

$$\begin{bmatrix} 0 & 1 & 0 & \ldots & 0 \\ 0 & 0 & 2 & \ldots & 0 \\ \vdots & \vdots & \vdots & \ddots & \vdots \\ 0 & 0 & 0 & \ldots & n \\ 0 & 0 & 0 & \ldots & 0 \end{bmatrix}.$$

It is natural to ask what are the matrices that represent sums and scalar multiples of linear mappings. The answer is as follows.

7.1 Theorem *If V, W are of dimensions m, n respectively and if $f, g : V \to W$ are linear then, relative to fixed ordered bases,*

$$\text{Mat}(f + g) = \text{Mat}\, f + \text{Mat}\, g$$

and, for every scalar λ,

$$\text{Mat}\, \lambda f = \lambda \, \text{Mat}\, f.$$

Proof Let $\text{Mat}\, f = [x_{ij}]_{n \times m}$ and $\text{Mat}\, g = [y_{ij}]_{n \times m}$ relative to the fixed ordered bases $(a_i)_m$ of V and $(b_i)_n$ of W. Then for $i = 1, \ldots, m$ we have

$$f(a_i) = \sum_{j=1}^{n} x_{ji} b_j, \qquad g(a_i) = \sum_{j=1}^{n} y_{ji} b_j.$$

Consequently, $(f + g)(a_i) = \sum_{j=1}^{n} (x_{ji} + y_{ji}) b_j$ and we have that

$$[\text{Mat}(f + g)]_{ji} = x_{ji} + y_{ji} = [\text{Mat}\, f + \text{Mat}\, g]_{ji}$$

whence $\text{Mat}(f + g) = \text{Mat}\, f + \text{Mat}\, g$. Similarly,

$$(\lambda f)(a_i) = \sum_{j=1}^{n} \lambda x_{ji} b_j$$

gives $[\text{Mat}\, \lambda f]_{ji} = \lambda x_{ji} = [\lambda \, \text{Mat}\, f]_{ji}$, so $\text{Mat}\, \lambda f = \lambda \, \text{Mat}\, f$. $\Diamond$

We can express 7.1 in an even neater way as follows. Consider the set $\text{Lin}(V, W)$ of linear mappings from a vector space V of dimension m to a vector space W of dimension n (each over the same field F). It is clear that $\text{Lin}(V, W)$ is a vector space. Consider now the mapping

$$\vartheta : \text{Lin}(V, W) \to \text{Mat}_{n \times m}(F)$$

given by $\vartheta(f) = \text{Mat}\, f$ where V and W are referred to fixed ordered bases $(v_i)_m$ and $(w_j)_n$ throughout. This mapping ϑ is surjective since, given any then we have $n \times m$ matrix $M = [m_{ij}]$, we can define

$$(i = 1, \ldots, m) \qquad f(v_i) = \sum_{j=1}^{n} m_{ji} w_j.$$

By 6.8 this produces a linear mapping $f : V \to W$, and clearly we have $\text{Mat}\, f = M$. Moreover, ϑ is injective; this is immediate from 6.10 and the definition of the matrix of a linear mapping. Thus ϑ is a bijection which, by 7.1, satisfies $\vartheta(f + g) = \vartheta(f) + \vartheta(g)$ and $\vartheta(\lambda f) = \lambda \, \vartheta(f)$. In other words, ϑ is a vector space isomorphism and we have :

7.2 Theorem *If V, W are of dimensions m, n respectively over F then*

$$\mathrm{Lin}(V, W) \simeq \mathrm{Mat}_{n \times m}(F). \ \diamond$$

It is reasonable to ask if, for given bases $(v_i)_m$ of V and $(w_i)_n$ of W, there is a 'natural' basis for the vector space $\mathrm{Lin}(V, W)$. Indeed there is, and this can be obtained from the natural basis

$$\{E_{pq} \ ; \ p = 1, \ldots, n \text{ and } q = 1, \ldots, m\}$$

of $\mathrm{Mat}_{n \times m}(F)$. If we define $f_{pq} : V \to W$ by setting

$$(i = 1, \ldots, m) \qquad f_{pq}(v_i) = \delta_{iq} w_p = \begin{cases} w_p & \text{if } i = q; \\ 0 & \text{otherwise,} \end{cases}$$

then we have

$$f_{pq}(v_1) = 0w_1 + \cdots + 0w_p + \cdots + 0w_n$$
$$\vdots$$
$$f_{pq}(v_q) = 0w_1 + \cdots + 1w_p + \cdots + 0w_n$$
$$\vdots$$
$$f_{pq}(v_m) = 0w_1 + \cdots + 0w_p + \cdots + 0w_n$$

and hence $\mathrm{Mat}\, f_{pq} = E_{pq}$, i.e. $\vartheta(f_{pq}) = E_{pq}$. Since the inverse of an isomorphism is also an isomorphism, it follows by 6.5 that a (natural) basis for $\mathrm{Lin}(V, W)$ is

$$\{f_{pq} \ ; \ p = 1, \ldots, n \text{ and } q = 1, \ldots, m\}.$$

We now turn our attention to the matrix that represents the composite of two linear mappings. It is precisely in investigating this that we shall see how the definition of matrix products arises in a very natural way.

Consider the following situation :

$$U; (u_i)_m \xrightarrow{\ f; A\ } V; (v_i)_n \xrightarrow{\ g; B\ } W; (w_i)_p$$

in which the notation $U; (u_i)_m$ for example denotes a vector space U with a fixed ordered basis $(u_i)_m$ and $f; A$ denotes a linear mapping f represented, relative to the fixed bases, by the matrix A.

The composite mapping is

$$U; (u_i)_m \xrightarrow{\quad g \circ f \quad} W; (w_i)_p.$$

What is the matrix of this composite? It is natural to expect that it depends on both A and B. That this is so is the substance of the following result.

7.3 Theorem $\mathrm{Mat}(g \circ f) = \mathrm{Mat}\, g \cdot \mathrm{Mat}\, f$.

Proof To find $\mathrm{Mat}(g \circ f)$ we have to express each $(g \circ f)(u_i)$ in terms of the basis $(w_i)_p$ of W. Now since $\mathrm{Mat}\, f = A$ we have

$$(i = 1, \ldots, m) \qquad f(u_i) = \sum_{j=1}^{n} a_{ji} v_j$$

and since $\mathrm{Mat}\, g = B$ we have

$$(j = 1, \ldots, n) \qquad g(v_j) = \sum_{k=1}^{p} b_{kj} w_k.$$

Thus, for each i,

$$\begin{aligned}
g[f(u_i)] = g\Big(\sum_{j=1}^{n} a_{ji} v_j\Big) &= \sum_{j=1}^{n} a_{ji} g(v_j) \\
&= \sum_{j=1}^{n} a_{ji} \Big(\sum_{k=1}^{p} b_{kj} w_k\Big) \\
&= \sum_{k=1}^{p} \Big(\sum_{j=1}^{n} b_{kj} a_{ji}\Big) w_k.
\end{aligned}$$

Consequently the (k, i)-th element of $\mathrm{Mat}(g \circ f)$ is $\sum_{j=1}^{n} b_{kj} a_{ji}$, which is the (k, i)-th element of $BA = \mathrm{Mat}\, g \cdot \mathrm{Mat}\, f$. $\Diamond$

7.4 Corollary *A square matrix is invertible if and only if it represents an isomorphism.*

Proof Suppose that A is an $n \times n$ matrix that is invertible. Then there is an $n \times n$ matrix B such that $BA = I_n$. Let V be a vector space of dimension n and let $(v_i)_n$ be a fixed ordered basis of V. If $f, g : V \to V$ are linear mappings that are represented, relative to this fixed ordered basis, by A, B respectively then by 7.3 we have that $g \circ f$ is represented by $BA = I_n$. It follows that $g \circ f = \text{id}_V$ whence f is an isomorphism by 6.5.

Conversely, if $f : V \to V$ is an isomorphism that is represented by the matrix A then the existence of $g : V \to V$ such that $g \circ f = \text{id}_V$ implies the existence of a matrix B (representing g) such that $BA = I_n$, whence A is invertible. $\diamond$

Example Consider $\mathbb{R}^3$ referred to the standard basis. If we change reference to the basis $\{(1, 1, 0), (1, 0, 1), (0, 1, 1)\}$ then the matrix of the identity mapping is obtained from

$$\text{id}(1, 0, 0) = (1, 0, 0) = \tfrac{1}{2}(1, 1, 0) + \tfrac{1}{2}(1, 0, 1) - \tfrac{1}{2}(0, 1, 1)$$
$$\text{id}(0, 1, 0) = (0, 1, 0) = \tfrac{1}{2}(1, 1, 0) - \tfrac{1}{2}(1, 0, 1) + \tfrac{1}{2}(0, 1, 1)$$
$$\text{id}(0, 0, 1) = (0, 0, 1) = -\tfrac{1}{2}(1, 1, 0) + \tfrac{1}{2}(1, 0, 1) + \tfrac{1}{2}(0, 1, 1)$$

i.e. it is

$$\tfrac{1}{2}\begin{bmatrix} 1 & 1 & -1 \\ 1 & -1 & 1 \\ -1 & 1 & 1 \end{bmatrix}.$$

Since the identity mapping is an isomorphism, this matrix is invertible.

The reader should note that it is to maintain the same order in which g, f appear in 7.3 that we choose to call the *transpose* of the coefficient matrix the matrix of the linear mapping. If, as some authors do, we were to write mappings on the right (i.e. write xf instead of $f(x)$) then this convention is unnecessary.

Suppose now that we have the situation

$$V; (v_i)_m \xrightarrow{\quad f; A \quad} W; (w_i)_n.$$

If we refer V to a new ordered basis $(v_i')_m$, and W to a new ordered basis $(w_i')_n$, then clearly the matrix that represents f will change. How does it change? We shall now address ourselves to this question.

First, consider the particular case where $W = V$ and $f = \text{id}_V$ (the identity mapping on V), so that we have the following situation :

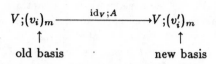

$$V;(v_i)_m \xrightarrow{\quad \text{id}_V\,;A \quad} V;(v_i')_m$$

old basis   new basis

Note that this is precisely the situation described in the previous Example. We call A the *transition matrix from the (old) basis* $(v_i)_m$ *to the (new) basis* $(v_i')_m$.

The following result is now clear from 7.4 :

7.5 Theorem *Transition matrices are invertible.* ◇

We can now describe how a change of bases is governed by the transition matrices that are involved.

7.6 Theorem [Change of bases] *If a linear mapping $f : V \to W$ is represented relative to ordered bases $(v_i)_m, (w_i)_n$ by the $n \times m$ matrix A then relative to new ordered bases $(v_i')_m, (w_i')_n$ the matrix representing f is the $n \times m$ matrix $Q^{-1}AP$ where Q is the transition matrix from $(w_i')_n$ to $(w_i)_n$ and P is the transition matrix from $(v_i')_m$ to $(v_i)_m$.*

Proof Using the notation introduced above, consider the diagram

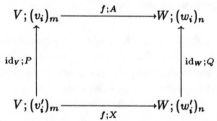

We have to determine the matrix X. Now this diagram is 'commutative' in the sense that travelling from the south-west corner to the north-east corner is independent of whichever route we choose, for clearly we have $f \circ \text{id}_V = \text{id}_W \circ f$. It therefore follows by 7.3 that the matrices representing these routes are equal, i.e. that $AP = QX$. But Q, being a transition matrix, is invertible by 7.5 and so we deduce that $X = Q^{-1}QX = Q^{-1}AP$. ◇

Example Suppose that $f : \mathbb{R}^3 \rightarrow \mathbb{R}^3$ is the linear mapping whose matrix relative to the standard ordered basis is

$$A = \begin{bmatrix} 2 & -3 & 1 \\ 3 & -2 & 0 \\ -4 & 1 & 2 \end{bmatrix}$$

and let us compute the matrix of f when $\mathbb{R}^3$ is referred to the ordered basis

$$B = \{(1, -1, 1), (1, -2, 2), (1, -2, 1)\}.$$

We apply 7.6 with $W = V = \mathbb{R}^3$, $(w_i) = (v_i) =$ the standard ordered basis, and $(w_i') = (v_i') =$ the new ordered basis B. The transition matrix from the new basis to the old ($=$standard) basis is

$$P = \begin{bmatrix} 1 & 1 & 1 \\ -1 & -2 & -2 \\ 1 & 2 & 1 \end{bmatrix}.$$

Note that this is obtained by simply taking the elements of B and turning them into the columns of P. This becomes clear on observing that we have

$$\text{id}(1, -1, 1) = (1, -1, 1) = 1(1, 0, 0) - 1(0, 1, 0) + 1(0, 0, 1)$$
$$\text{id}(1, -2, 2) = (1, -2, 2) = 1(1, 0, 0) - 2(0, 1, 0) + 2(0, 0, 1)$$
$$\text{id}(1, -2, 1) = (1, -2, 1) = 1(1, 0, 0) - 2(0, 1, 0) + 1(0, 0, 1)$$

and the transition matrix P is the transpose of this coefficient matrix.

Now P is invertible, and the reader can verify that

$$P^{-1} = \begin{bmatrix} 2 & 1 & 0 \\ -1 & 0 & 1 \\ 0 & -1 & -1 \end{bmatrix}.$$

The matrix of f relative to the new basis B is then

$$P^{-1}AP = \begin{bmatrix} 17 & 27 & 25 \\ -9 & -12 & -13 \\ -2 & -5 & -3 \end{bmatrix}.$$

Example Relative to the bases $\{(1,0,-1),(0,2,0),(1,2,3)\}$ of $\mathbb{R}^3$ and $\{(-1,1),(2,0)\}$ of $\mathbb{R}^2$, suppose that the linear mapping $f : \mathbb{R}^3 \to \mathbb{R}^2$ is represented by the matrix

$$A = \begin{bmatrix} 2 & -1 & 3 \\ 3 & 1 & 0 \end{bmatrix}.$$

To find the matrices that represent f relative to the standard bases we first determine the transition matrices P, Q from the standard bases to the given bases. Making use of the observation in the previous Example, we can say immediately that

$$Q^{-1} = \begin{bmatrix} -1 & 2 \\ 1 & 0 \end{bmatrix}, \qquad P^{-1} = \begin{bmatrix} 1 & 0 & 1 \\ 0 & 2 & 2 \\ -1 & 0 & 3 \end{bmatrix}.$$

The reader can verify that

$$P = \tfrac{1}{8} \begin{bmatrix} 6 & 0 & -2 \\ -2 & 4 & -2 \\ 2 & 0 & 2 \end{bmatrix}$$

and hence that the required matrix is

$$Q^{-1}AP = \tfrac{1}{2} \begin{bmatrix} 3 & 3 & -5 \\ 5 & -1 & 1 \end{bmatrix}.$$

We now establish the converse of 7.6.

7.7 Theorem *Let $(v_i)_m, (w_i)_n$ be ordered bases of vector spaces V, W respectively. Suppose that A, B are $n \times m$ matrices such that there are invertible matrices P, Q with $B = Q^{-1}AP$. Then there are ordered bases $(v_i')_m, (w_i')_n$ of V, W and a linear mapping $f : V \to W$ such that A is the matrix of f relative to $(v_i)_m, (w_i)_n$ and B is the matrix of f relative to $(v_i')_m, (w_i')_n$.*

Proof If $P = [p_{ij}]_{m \times m}$ and $Q = [q_{ij}]_{n \times n}$ define

$$(i = 1, \ldots, m) \qquad v_i' = \sum_{j=1}^{m} p_{ji} v_j\,;$$

$$(i = 1, \ldots, n) \qquad w_i' = \sum_{j=1}^{n} q_{ji} w_j\,.$$

Since P is invertible there is, by 7.4, an isomorphism $f_P : V \to V$ that is represented by P relative to the ordered basis $(v_i)_m$. Since by definition $v_i' = f_P(v_i)$ for each i, it follows that $(v_i')_m$ is an ordered basis of V and that P is the transition matrix from $(v_i')_m$ to $(v_i)_m$. Similarly, $(w_i')_n$ is an ordered basis of W and Q is the transition matrix from $(w_i')_n$ to $(w_i)_n$.

Now let $f : V \to W$ be the linear mapping whose matrix, relative to the ordered bases $(v_i)_m$ and $(w_i)_n$ is A. Then by 7.6 the matrix of f relative to the ordered bases $(v_i')_m$ and $(w_i')_n$ is $Q^{-1}AP = B.$ $\diamond$

In the proof of 3.16 we observed that a matrix A of rank p can be transformed by means of row and column operations to the form

$$\begin{bmatrix} I_p & 0 \\ 0 & 0 \end{bmatrix}.$$

We can also deduce this as follows from the results we have established for linear mappings.

Let V, W be of dimensions m, n respectively and let $f : V \to W$ be a linear map with $\dim \operatorname{Im} f = p$. By 6.4 we have

$$\dim \operatorname{Ker} f = \dim V - \dim \operatorname{Im} f = m - p,$$

so let $\{v_1, \ldots, v_{m-p}\}$ be a basis of $\operatorname{Ker} f$. Extend this (5.10) to a basis

$$B = \{u_1, \ldots, u_p, v_1, \ldots, v_{m-p}\}$$

of V. Observe now that $\{f(u_1), \ldots, f(u_p)\}$ is linearly independent; for if $\sum_{i=1}^{p} \lambda_i f(u_i) = 0$ then $f\left(\sum_{i=1}^{p} \lambda_i u_i\right) = 0$ so $\sum_{i=1}^{p} \lambda_i u_i \in$ $\operatorname{Ker} f$ whence $\sum_{i=1}^{p} \lambda_i u_i = \sum_{j=1}^{m-p} \mu_j v_j$. Then $\sum_{i=1}^{p} \lambda_i u_i - \sum_{j=1}^{m-p} \mu_j v_j = 0$ and consequently every λ_i and every μ_j is 0. It follows by 5.11 that $\{f(u_1), \ldots, f(u_p)\}$ is a basis of the subspace $\operatorname{Im} f$. Now extend this (5.10) to a basis

$$C = \{f(u_1), \ldots, f(u_p), w_1, \ldots, w_{n-p}\}$$

of W. Then we have

$$f(u_1) = 1f(u_1) + 0f(u_2) + \cdots + 0f(u_p) + \cdots + 0w_{n-p}$$
$$f(u_2) = 0f(u_1) + 1f(u_2) + \cdots + 0f(u_p) + \cdots + 0w_{n-p}$$
$$\vdots$$
$$f(u_p) = 0f(u_1) + 0f(u_2) + \cdots + 1f(u_p) + \cdots + 0w_{n-p}$$
$$f(v_1) = 0f(u_1) + 0f(u_2) + \cdots + 0f(u_p) + \cdots + 0w_{n-p}$$
$$\vdots$$
$$f(v_{m-p}) = 0f(u_1) + 0f(u_2) + \cdots + 0f(u_p) + \cdots + 0w_{n-p}$$

since $f(v_1) = \cdots = f(v_{m-p}) = 0$. The matrix of f relative to the bases B, C is then

$$\begin{bmatrix} I_p & 0 \\ 0 & 0 \end{bmatrix},$$

where p is the rank of f.

Suppose now that A is a given $n \times m$ matrix. If, relative to fixed ordered bases B_V, B_W this matrix represents the linear mapping $f : V \to W$ then, Q and P being the appropriate transition matrices from the bases B, C to the fixed bases B_V and B_W, we have

$$Q^{-1}AP = \begin{bmatrix} I_p & 0 \\ 0 & 0 \end{bmatrix}.$$

Now since transition matrices are invertible they are products of elementary matrices. This means, therefore, that A can be reduced by means of row and column operations to the form

$$\begin{bmatrix} I_p & 0 \\ 0 & 0 \end{bmatrix}.$$

The above discussion shows, incidentally, that *the rank of a linear mapping f is the same as the rank of any matrix that represents f.*

Definition If A, B are $n \times n$ matrices then B is said to be *similar* to A if there is an invertible matrix P such that $B = P^{-1}AP$.

It is clear that if B is similar to A then A is similar to B (for then $A = PBP^{-1} = (P^{-1})^{-1}AP^{-1}$), and that if B is similar to A and C is similar to B then $B = P^{-1}AP$ and $C = Q^{-1}BQ$ give $C = Q^{-1}P^{-1}APQ = (PQ)^{-1}APQ$, so that C is similar to A. Thus the relation of being similar is an equivalence relation on the set of $n \times n$ matrices.

The importance of the notion of similar matrices is reflected in the following result.

7.8 Theorem *Two $n \times n$ matrices A, B are similar if and only if they represent the same linear mapping relative to possibly different ordered bases.*

Proof This is immediate from 7.6 and 7.7 on taking $W = V$ and, for every i, $w_i = v_i$ and $w_i' = v_i'$. $\diamond$

7.9 Corollary *Similar matrices have the same rank.* $\diamond$

The notion of similar matrices brings us back in a more concrete way to the discussion, at the end of Chapter Four, concerning the problem of deciding when (in our new terminology) a square matrix is similar to a diagonal matrix; equivalently, when a linear mapping can be represented by a diagonal matrix. We are not in a position to answer this question, but will proceed in the next Chapter to develop some machinery that will help us towards this objective.

CHAPTER EIGHT

Determinants

In what follows it will prove convenient to write an $n \times n$ matrix A in the form

$$A = [a_1, a_2, \ldots, a_n]$$

where, as before, the notation a_i represents the i-th column of A. Also, the letter F will signify as usual either the field $\mathbb{R}$ of real numbers or the field $\mathbb{C}$ of complex numbers.

Definition A mapping $D : \text{Mat}_{n \times n}(F) \to F$ is said to be *determinantal* if it satisfies the properties

(1) $D[\ldots, b_i + c_i, \ldots] = D[\ldots, b_i, \ldots] + D[\ldots, c_i, \ldots]$;

(2) $D[\ldots, \lambda a_i, \ldots] = \lambda D[\ldots, a_i, \ldots]$;

(3) $D[a_1, \ldots, a_i, \ldots, a_j, \ldots, a_n] = -D[\ldots, a_j, \ldots, a_i, \ldots]$;

(4) $D(I_n) = 1$.

Note that (1) and (2) may be expressed by saying that D is a linear function of the i-th column for $i = 1, \ldots, n$; equivalently, that D is *multilinear*. Also, (3) may be described by saying that $D(A)$ changes in sign when two columns of A are interchanged; equivalently, that D is *alternating*.

8.1 Theorem *If D is a mapping that satisfies property* (1) *then D satisfies property* (3) *if and only if it satisfies the property*

(3') $D(A) = 0$ *whenever A has two identical columns.*

Proof Taking $a_i = a_j$ with $i \neq j$ in (3) we obtain $D(A) = -D(A)$ whence $D(A) = 0$ and so (3) $\Rightarrow$ (3').

Suppose now that D satisfies (1) and (3'). Then

$$
\begin{aligned}
0 &= D[\ldots, \mathbf{a}_i + \mathbf{a}_j, \ldots, \mathbf{a}_i + \mathbf{a}_j, \ldots] \\
&= D[\ldots, \mathbf{a}_i, \ldots, \mathbf{a}_i + \mathbf{a}_j, \ldots] + D[\ldots, \mathbf{a}_j, \ldots, \mathbf{a}_i + \mathbf{a}_j, \ldots] \\
&= D[\ldots, \mathbf{a}_i, \ldots, \mathbf{a}_i, \ldots] + D[\ldots, \mathbf{a}_i, \ldots, \mathbf{a}_j, \ldots] \\
&\qquad + D[\ldots, \mathbf{a}_j, \ldots, \mathbf{a}_i, \ldots] + D[\ldots, \mathbf{a}_j, \ldots, \mathbf{a}_j, \ldots] \\
&= D[\ldots, \mathbf{a}_i, \ldots, \mathbf{a}_j, \ldots] + D[\ldots, \mathbf{a}_j, \ldots, \mathbf{a}_i, \ldots]
\end{aligned}
$$

whence (3) follows. $\diamondsuit$

8.2 Corollary *D is determinantal if and only if it satisfies the properties* $(1), (2), (3'), (4)$. $\diamondsuit$

Example Let $D : \mathrm{Mat}_{2\times 2}(\mathbb{R}) \to \mathbb{R}$ be given by

$$
D \begin{bmatrix} a_{11} & a_{12} \\ a_{21} & a_{22} \end{bmatrix} = a_{11}a_{22} - a_{12}a_{21}.
$$

Then it is an easy exercise to show that D satisfies properties (1) to (4) above, so that D is determinantal.

Suppose now that $f : \mathrm{Mat}_{2\times 2}(\mathbb{R}) \to \mathbb{R}$ is a determinantal mapping. Writing

$$
\delta_1 = \begin{bmatrix} 1 \\ 0 \end{bmatrix}, \qquad \delta_2 = \begin{bmatrix} 0 \\ 1 \end{bmatrix},
$$

we see that every $A \in \mathrm{Mat}_{2\times 2}(\mathbb{R})$ can be expressed as

$$
A = [a_{11}\delta_1 + a_{21}\delta_2, \; a_{12}\delta_1 + a_{22}\delta_2]
$$

so that, by property (1),

$$
f(A) = f[a_{11}\delta_1, a_{12}\delta_1 + a_{22}\delta_2] + f[a_{21}\delta_2, a_{12}\delta_1 + a_{22}\delta_2].
$$

By applying (1) again, the first summand can be expanded to

$$
f[a_{11}\delta_1, a_{12}\delta_1] + f[a_{11}\delta_1, a_{22}\delta_2]
$$

which, by (2), is

$$
a_{11}a_{12}f[\delta_1, \delta_1] + a_{11}a_{22}f[\delta_1, \delta_2].
$$

Applying (4) and 8.1, we see that this reduces to $a_{11}a_{22}$.

As for the second summand, by (1) this can be expanded to

$$f[a_{21}\delta_2, a_{12}\delta_1] + f[a_{21}\delta_2, a_{22}\delta_2],$$

which, by (2) is

$$a_{21}a_{12}f[\delta_2, \delta_1] + a_{21}a_{22}f[\delta_2, \delta_2].$$

Applying (3),(4) and 8.1, we see that this reduces to $-a_{21}a_{12}$.

Thus $f(A) = a_{11}a_{22} - a_{12}a_{21}$ and we observe that f coincides with the determinantal mapping D described in the above Example. Clearly, the same is true if we replace $\mathbb{R}$ by $\mathbb{C}$, and so we have proved that that *there is a unique determinantal mapping on* $\mathrm{Mat}_{2\times 2}(F)$.

Our objective in what follows will be to extend this observation to $\mathrm{Mat}_{n\times n}(F)$ for every positive integer n. The case where $n = 1$ is of course trivial : if $A = [a]$ then it is clear that the only determinantal mapping is given by $D(A) = a$.

If $A \in \mathrm{Mat}_{n\times n}(F)$ then we shall use the notation A_{ij} to denote the $(n-1) \times (n-1)$ matrix that is obtained from A by deleting the i-th row and the j-th column of A (i.e. the row and column containing a_{ij}).

The following result shows how we can construct determinantal mappings on the set of $n \times n$ matrices from a given determinantal mapping on the set of $(n-1) \times (n-1)$ matrices.

8.3 Theorem *For $n > 1$ let $D : \mathrm{Mat}_{(n-1)\times(n-1)}(F) \to F$ be determinantal, and for $i = 1,\ldots,n$ define $f_i : \mathrm{Mat}_{n\times n}(F) \to F$ by*

$$f_i(A) = \sum_{j=1}^{n} (-1)^{i+j} a_{ij} D(A_{ij}).$$

Then each f_i is determinantal.

Proof It is clear that $D(A_{ij})$ is independent of the j-th column of A and so $a_{ij}D(A_{ij})$ depends linearly on the j-th column of A. Consequently we see that f_i depends linearly on the columns of A, i.e. satisfies conditions (1) and (2) of the definition of a determinantal mapping.

We now show that f_i satisfies condition (3'). Suppose that A has two identical columns, say the p-th and the q-th columns (with $p \neq q$). Now for $j \neq p$ and $j \neq q$ the $(n-1) \times (n-1)$ matrix A_{ij} has two identical columns and so, since D is determinantal by hypothesis, we have

$$(j \neq p, q) \qquad D(A_{ij}) = 0.$$

It follows that the expression for $f_i(A)$ reduces to

$$f_i(A) = (-1)^{i+p} a_{ip} D(A_{ip}) + (-1)^{i+q} a_{iq} D(A_{iq}).$$

Suppose, without loss of generality, that $p < q$. Then it is clear that A_{iq} can be transformed into A_{ip} by effecting $q - 1 - p$ interchanges of adjacent columns; so, by property (3),

$$D(A_{iq}) = (-1)^{q-1-p} D(A_{ip}).$$

Since $a_{ip} = a_{iq}$ we thus have

$$f_i(A) = [(-1)^{i+p} + (-1)^{i+q}(-1)^{q-1-p}] a_{ip} D(A_{ip})$$

which reduces to 0 since

$$\begin{aligned}
(-1)^{i+p} + (-1)^{i+q}(-1)^{q-1-p} &= (-1)^{i+p}[1 + (-1)^{2q-2p-1}] \\
&= (-1)^{i+p}[1 + (-1)] \\
&= 0.
\end{aligned}$$

Finally, f_i satisfies property (4) since if $A = I_n$ then $a_{ij} = \delta_{ij}$ and $A_{ii} = I_{n-1}$, so that

$$f_i(I_n) = (-1)^{i+i} \delta_{ii} D(I_{n-1}) = 1.$$

It now follows by 8.2 that f_i is determinantal for every i. $\diamond$

8.4 Corollary *For every positive integer n there is at least one determinantal mapping on* $\text{Mat}_{n \times n}(F)$.

Proof Proceed by induction. The result is trivial for $n = 1$, and 8.3 shows how at least one such mapping can be defined on $\text{Mat}_{n \times n}(F)$ from a given determinantal mapping on $\text{Mat}_{(n-1) \times (n-1)}(F)$. $\diamond$

Our objective now is to establish the uniqueness of a determinantal mapping on $\mathrm{Mat}_{n \times n}(F)$. For this purpose, we recall that a *transposition* on the set $\{1, \ldots, n\}$ is a permutation (=bijection) τ on $\{1, \ldots, n\}$ such that, for some i, j with $i \neq j$,

$$\tau(i) = j, \quad \tau(j) = i, \quad \text{and} \quad (\forall x \neq i, j) \; \tau(x) = x.$$

In other words, a transposition is a bijection that interchanges two elements (i and j) and 'fixes' the other elements. The set of permutations on $\{1, \ldots, n\}$ is denoted by P_n. For every $\sigma \in P_n$ we define the *signum* ε_σ of σ by

$$\varepsilon_\sigma = \prod_{i < j} \frac{\sigma(j) - \sigma(i)}{j - i}.$$

The following theorem lists results that we shall require concerning permutations and transpositions; these can be found, for example, in Volume One.

8.5 Theorem (1) *If $n \geq 2$ then every $\sigma \in P_n$ can be expressed as a composite of transpositions;*
(2) *If $\tau \in P_n$ is a transposition then $\varepsilon_\tau = -1$;*
(3) $(\forall \sigma, \vartheta \in P_n) \quad \varepsilon_{\sigma \circ \vartheta} = \varepsilon_\sigma \varepsilon_\vartheta.$ $\Diamond$

8.6 Corollary *If $\sigma \in P_n$ then $\varepsilon_\sigma = \pm 1$ and $\varepsilon_{\sigma^{-1}} = \varepsilon_\sigma$.* $\Diamond$

Using these results we can now prove :

8.7 Theorem *There is one and only one determinantal mapping $D : \mathrm{Mat}_{n \times n}(F) \to F$, and it can be described by*

$$D(A) = \sum_{\sigma \in P_n} \varepsilon_\sigma \, a_{\sigma(1),1} \cdots a_{\sigma(n),n}.$$

Proof We know by 8.4 that a determinantal mapping D exists on $\mathrm{Mat}_{n \times n}(F)$. If we write δ_j for the j-th column of I_n then we can represent an $n \times n$ matrix $A = [a_{ij}]$ by

$$[a_{11}\delta_1 + \cdots + a_{n1}\delta_n, \; \ldots \ldots, \; a_{1n}\delta_1 + \cdots + a_{nn}\delta_n].$$

Using property (1) in the definition of a determinantal mapping we can write $D(A)$ as a sum of terms of the form

$$D[a_{\sigma(1),1}\delta_{\sigma(1)}, \ldots, a_{\sigma(n),n}\delta_{\sigma(n)}],$$

where $1 \leq \sigma(i) \leq n$ for every i. Using property (2) we can then write each of these terms as

$$a_{\sigma(1),1} \cdots a_{\sigma(n),n} \, D[\delta_{\sigma(1)}, \ldots, \delta_{\sigma(n)}].$$

But by (3′) each such expression is 0 except for those in which $\sigma(i) \neq \sigma(j)$ for $i \neq j$; i.e. those in which σ is a permutation on $\{1, \ldots, n\}$. Thus we have that

$$D(A) = \sum_{\sigma \in P_n} a_{\sigma(1),1} \cdots a_{\sigma(n),n} \, D[\delta_{\sigma(1)}, \ldots, \delta_{\sigma(n)}].$$

Now the columns $\delta_{\sigma(1)}, \ldots, \delta_{\sigma(n)}$ occur in the permutation σ of the standard arrangement $\delta_1, \ldots, \delta_n$. If $\sigma = \tau_1 \circ \cdots \circ \tau_k$ where each τ_i is a transposition then we have $\sigma^{-1} = \tau_k^{-1} \circ \cdots \circ \tau_1^{-1}$. Restoring the standard arrangement of the columns by applying in turn $\tau_1^{-1}, \ldots, \tau_k^{-1}$ we see from property (3) and the fact that $\varepsilon_{\sigma^{-1}} = \varepsilon_\sigma$ that

$$D[\delta_{\sigma(1)}, \ldots, \delta_{\sigma(n)}] = \varepsilon_\sigma \, D[\delta_1, \ldots, \delta_n].$$

We can now use property (4) to conclude that

$$D(A) = \sum_{\sigma \in P_n} \varepsilon_\sigma \, a_{\sigma(1),1} \cdots a_{\sigma(n),n}.$$

The above argument also shows that D is unique. $\Diamond$

An important consequence of the above result is that *the expression for $f_i(A)$ given in 8.3 is independent of i.*

Definition The unique determinantal mapping on $\mathrm{Mat}_{n \times n}(F)$ will be denoted by det. By the *determinant* of $A = [a_{ij}]_{n \times n}$ we shall mean det A.

By 8.7 we have that

$$\det A = \sum_{\sigma \in P_n} \varepsilon_\sigma \, a_{\sigma(1),1} \cdots a_{\sigma(n),n}.$$

Alternatively, by 8.3, we have that

$$\det A = \sum_{j=1}^{n} (-1)^{i+j} a_{ij} \det A_{ij},$$

which is called the *Laplace expansion along the i-th row*. Note that it is independent of the row chosen.

Example Consider the matrix

$$A = \begin{bmatrix} 1 & 1 & -1 \\ 2 & 1 & 3 \\ 1 & -5 & 1 \end{bmatrix}.$$

Using a Laplace expansion along the first row we have

$$\det A = 1.\det \begin{bmatrix} 1 & 3 \\ -5 & 1 \end{bmatrix} - 1.\det \begin{bmatrix} 2 & 3 \\ 1 & 1 \end{bmatrix} + (-1).\det \begin{bmatrix} 2 & 1 \\ 1 & -5 \end{bmatrix}$$

$$= 16 - (-1) - (-11)$$

$$= 28.$$

Expanding along the second row, we obtain

$$\det A = -2.\det \begin{bmatrix} 1 & -1 \\ -5 & 1 \end{bmatrix} + 1.\det \begin{bmatrix} 1 & -1 \\ 1 & 1 \end{bmatrix} - 3.\det \begin{bmatrix} 1 & 1 \\ 1 & -5 \end{bmatrix}$$

$$= -2(-4) + 2 - 3(-6)$$

$$= 28.$$

Finally, expanding along the third row we obtain

$$\det A = 1.\det \begin{bmatrix} 1 & -1 \\ 1 & 3 \end{bmatrix} - (-5).\det \begin{bmatrix} 1 & -1 \\ 2 & 3 \end{bmatrix} + 1.\det \begin{bmatrix} 1 & 1 \\ 2 & 1 \end{bmatrix}$$

$$= 4 + 5 \cdot 5 + (-1)$$

$$= 28.$$

8.8 Theorem *For every square matrix A, $\det A = \det A^t$.*

Proof If $\sigma \in P_n$ then whenever $\sigma(i) = j$ we have $i = \sigma^{-1}(j)$ and so $a_{\sigma(i),i} = a_{j,\sigma^{-1}(j)}$. Consequently

$$a_{\sigma(1),1} \cdots a_{\sigma(n),n} = a_{1,\sigma^{-1}(1)} \cdots a_{n,\sigma^{-1}(n)}$$
$$= [A^t]_{\sigma^{-1}(1),1} \cdots [A^t]_{\sigma^{-1}(n),n}.$$

Now as σ ranges over P_n so does σ^{-1}; and $\varepsilon_\sigma = \varepsilon_{\sigma^{-1}}$. Thus

$$\det A = \sum_{\sigma \in P_n} \varepsilon_\sigma a_{\sigma(1),1} \cdots a_{\sigma(n),n}$$
$$= \sum_{\sigma^{-1} \in P_n} \varepsilon_{\sigma^{-1}} [A^t]_{\sigma^{-1}(1),1} \cdots [A^t]_{\sigma^{-1}(n),n}$$
$$= \det A^t. \quad \Diamond$$

8.9 Corollary $(j = 1,\dots,n) \quad \det A = \sum_{i=1}^{n} (-1)^{i+j} a_{ij} \det A_{ij}.$

Proof We have

$$\det A = \det A^t = \sum_{j=1}^{n} (-1)^{i+j} a_{ji} \det A_{ji}$$

$$= \sum_{i=1}^{n} (-1)^{i+j} a_{ij} \det A_{ij},$$

the second summation being obtained from the first by interchanging i and j. ◇

The reader should note carefully that in 8.9 the summation is over the first index. Thus we can assert that *Laplace expansions along the columns of A are also valid.* The reader can easily check that when column expansions are applied to the previous Example the same results are obtained.

It is useful to know how row and column operations affect the determinant of a square matrix. It is clear from property (3) in the definition of a determinantal mapping that if B is obtained from A by interchanging two columns then $\det B = -\det A$; and from property (2) that if B is obtained from A by multiplying a column of A by a scalar λ then $\det B = \lambda \det A$. Finally, if B is obtained from A by adding, say, λ times the i-th column to the j-th column then, by properties (1) and (3'),

$$\det B = \det[\dots, \mathbf{a}_i, \dots, \mathbf{a}_j + \lambda \mathbf{a}_i, \dots]$$

$$= \det[\dots, \mathbf{a}_i, \dots, \mathbf{a}_j, \dots] + \det[\dots, \mathbf{a}_i, \dots, \lambda \mathbf{a}_i, \dots]$$

$$= \det A + \lambda \det[\dots, \mathbf{a}_i, \dots, \mathbf{a}_i, \dots]$$

$$= \det A + \lambda.0$$

$$= \det A.$$

Since row operations on A are simply column operations on A^t and $\det A^t = \det A$, it is clear that similar observations hold for row operations.

Example Consider again the matrix

$$A = \begin{bmatrix} 1 & 1 & -1 \\ 2 & 1 & 3 \\ 1 & -5 & 1 \end{bmatrix}.$$

Using row operations we have

$$\det A = \det \begin{bmatrix} 1 & 1 & -1 \\ 0 & -1 & 5 \\ 0 & -6 & 2 \end{bmatrix} \begin{matrix} \\ \rho_2 - 2\rho_1 \\ \rho_3 - \rho_1 \end{matrix}$$

$$= \det \begin{bmatrix} -1 & 5 \\ -6 & 2 \end{bmatrix}$$

$$= -2 + 30$$

$$= 28.$$

Example For the matrix

$$A = \begin{bmatrix} 1 & -1 & 2 & 3 \\ 2 & 2 & 0 & 2 \\ 1 & 2 & 3 & 0 \\ 5 & 3 & 2 & -1 \end{bmatrix}$$

we have

$$\det A = \det \begin{bmatrix} 1 & -1 & 2 & 3 \\ 0 & 4 & -4 & -4 \\ 0 & 3 & 1 & -3 \\ 0 & 8 & -8 & -16 \end{bmatrix} \begin{matrix} \\ \rho_2 - 2\rho_1 \\ \rho_3 - \rho_1 \\ \rho_4 - 5\rho_1 \end{matrix}$$

$$= \det \begin{bmatrix} 4 & -4 & -4 \\ 3 & 1 & -3 \\ 8 & -8 & -16 \end{bmatrix}$$

$$= 4 \cdot 8 \cdot \det \begin{bmatrix} 1 & -1 & -1 \\ 3 & 1 & -3 \\ 1 & -1 & -2 \end{bmatrix}$$

$$= 32 \det \begin{bmatrix} 1 & -1 & -1 \\ 0 & 4 & 0 \\ 0 & 0 & -1 \end{bmatrix} \begin{matrix} \\ \rho_2 - 3\rho_1 \\ \rho_3 - \rho_1 \end{matrix}$$

$$= 32(-4)$$

$$= -128.$$

There are other methods of evaluating determinants that are useful, depending on the matrices involved. For example, there is the so-called 'inspection method' which is illustrated in the following examples.

Example Consider the matrix

$$A = \begin{bmatrix} 1 & x & x^2 \\ 1 & y & y^2 \\ 1 & z & z^2 \end{bmatrix}.$$

Observe that if we set $x = y$ then the first two rows are equal and so the determinant of A reduces to zero. Thus $x - y$ is a factor of det A. Similarly, so are $x - z$ and $y - z$. Now the highest power of x, y, z appearing in the $\sum_{\sigma}$-expansion is 2 (for every term in the expansion is a product of entries in distinct rows and columns). Consequently we can say that

$$\det A = k(x - y)(y - z)(z - x)$$

for some constant k. To determine k, observe that the product yz^2 of the diagonal entries is a term in the $\sum_{\sigma}$-expansion (namely, that corresponding to the identity permutation). But the term involving yz^2 in the above expression for det A is kyz^2. Thus we see that $k = 1$ and $\det A = (x - y)(y - z)(z - x)$.

Example Consider the matrix

$$A = \begin{bmatrix} a & b & c & d \\ a^2 & b^2 & c^2 & d^2 \\ b+c+d & c+d+a & d+a+b & a+b+c \\ bcd & cda & dab & abc \end{bmatrix}.$$

By the 'inspection method', factors of det A are

$$a - b, \ a - c, \ a - d, \ b - c, \ b - d, \ c - d.$$

The product of the diagonal entries, namely $a^2 b^3 c(d+a+b)$, is a term in the $\sum_{\sigma}$-expansion. But this is only partially represented in the product

$$(a - \underline{b})(\underline{a} - c)(\underline{a} - d)(\underline{b} - c)(\underline{b} - d)(\underline{c} - d),$$

which suggests that we have to find another factor. This can be discovered by adding row 1 to row 3 : clearly, this produces the factor $a + b + c + d$. Thus we have

$$\det A = k(a - b)(a - c)(a - d)(b - c)(b - d)(c - d)(a + b + c + d)$$

for some constant k; and comparing this with the diagonal product $a^2 b^3 c(d + a + b)$ we see that $k = -1$.

Example Consider the matrix

$$A = \begin{bmatrix} x & 1 & a & b \\ y^2 & y & 1 & c \\ yz^2 & z^2 & z & 1 \\ yzt & zt & t & 1 \end{bmatrix}.$$

If $x = y$ then the first column is y times the second column whence the determinant is 0 and so $x - y$ is a factor. If $z = t$ then the third and fourth rows are the same, so $z - t$ is a factor of det A. If now $y = z$ then we have

$$\det A = \det \begin{bmatrix} x & 1 & a & b \\ z^2 & z & 1 & c \\ z^3 & z^2 & z & 1 \\ z^2t & zt & t & 1 \end{bmatrix}$$

$$= \det \begin{bmatrix} x & 1 & a & b \\ z^2 & z & 1 & c \\ z^3 & z^2 & z & 1 \\ 0 & 0 & 0 & 1-tc \end{bmatrix}$$

$$= (1 - tc) \det \begin{bmatrix} x & 1 & a \\ z^2 & z & 1 \\ z^3 & z^2 & z \end{bmatrix}$$

$$= 0 \quad \text{since } \rho_3 = z\rho_2.$$

Thus we see that $y - z$ is also a factor. It now follows that

$$\det A = k(x - y)(y - z)(z - t)$$

for some constant k, and comparison with the product of the diagonal entries gives $k = 1$.

We now consider some further important properties of determinants.

8.10 Theorem *If* $A, B \in \text{Mat}_{n \times n}(F)$ *then*

$$\det AB = \det A \cdot \det B.$$

Proof If $C = AB$ then the k-th column of C can be written

$$\mathbf{c}_k = b_{1k}\mathbf{a}_1 + \cdots + b_{nk}\mathbf{a}_n.$$

To see this, observe that the i-th entry of $\mathbf{c}_k$ is

$$[\mathbf{c}_k]_i = c_{ik} = \sum_{j=1}^{n} a_{ij}b_{jk} = \sum_{j=1}^{n} b_{jk}[\mathbf{a}_j]_i = \Big[\sum_{j=1}^{n} b_{jk}\mathbf{a}_j\Big]_i.$$

Thus we have that

$$\det AB = \det C$$

$$= \det[b_{11}\mathbf{a}_1 + \cdots + b_{n1}\mathbf{a}_n, \ \ldots \ , b_{1n}\mathbf{a}_1 + \cdots + b_{nn}\mathbf{a}_n]$$

$$= \sum_{\sigma \in P_n} \det[b_{\sigma(1),1}\mathbf{a}_{\sigma(1)}, \ldots, b_{\sigma(n),n}\mathbf{a}_{\sigma(n)}]$$

$$= \sum_{\sigma \in P_n} b_{\sigma(1),1} \cdots b_{\sigma(n),n} \det[\mathbf{a}_{\sigma(1)}, \ldots, \mathbf{a}_{\sigma(n)}]$$

$$= \sum_{\sigma \in P_n} b_{\sigma(1),1} \cdots b_{\sigma(n),n} \, \varepsilon_\sigma \det[\mathbf{a}_1, \ldots, \mathbf{a}_n]$$

$$= \det A \cdot \sum_{\sigma \in P_n} \varepsilon_\sigma \, b_{\sigma(1),1} \cdots b_{\sigma(n),n}$$

$$= \det A \cdot \det B. \qquad \Diamond$$

Definition If $A \in \mathrm{Mat}_{n \times n}(F)$ we define the *adjugate* of A to be the $n \times n$ matrix $\mathrm{adj}\, A$ given by

$$[\mathrm{adj}\, A]_{ij} = (-1)^{i+j} \det A_{ji}.$$

It is very important to note the reversal of the suffices in the above definition. The adjugate matrix has the following useful property.

8.11 Theorem $A \cdot \mathrm{adj}\, A = (\det A)I_n.$

Proof We have

$$[A \cdot \mathrm{adj}\, A]_{ij} = \sum_{k=1}^{n} a_{ik}[\mathrm{adj}\, A]_{kj}$$

$$= \sum_{k=1}^{n} (-1)^{j+k} a_{ik} \det A_{jk}$$

$$= \begin{cases} \det A & \text{if } i = j; \\ 0 & \text{if } i \neq j, \end{cases}$$

Handwritten annotations in right margin:

By dy.

$\left(\det A = \sum (-1)^{i+j} a_{ij} \det A_{ij} \right)$

So if $i = j$ by df

$\sum (-1)^{j+k} a_{ik} \det A_{jk} =$

$a_{ik} \det A_{ik} = A$

the last equality resulting from the fact that when $i \neq j$ the expression represents the determinant of a matrix whose j-th row is equal to its i-th row. ◇

The reader should note that the matrix $(\det A)I_n$ is a diagonal matrix in which every entry on the diagonal is the scalar $\det A$.

We can use the above result to obtain a convenient way of determining whether or not a given square matrix is invertible, and a new way of computing inverses.

8.12 Theorem *A square matrix A is invertible if and only if $\det A \neq 0$, in which case the inverse is given by*

$$A^{-1} = \frac{1}{\det A} \, \text{adj} \, A.$$

Proof If $\det A \neq 0$ then by 8.11 we have

$$A \cdot \frac{1}{\det A} \text{adj} \, A = I_n$$

whence A^{-1} exists and is given by $\frac{1}{\det A} \text{adj} \, A$. Conversely, if A^{-1} exists then by 8.10 we have

$$1 = \det I_n = \det AA^{-1} = \det A \cdot \det A^{-1}$$

from which it is clear that $\det A \neq 0$. ◇

The result discovered in 8.12 provides a new way to compute inverses of matrices. In purely numerical examples, one can become quite skilful in its use. However, the adjugate matrix has to be constructed with some care! In particular, one should note the factor $(-1)^{i+j} = \pm 1$. The sign is given according to the scheme

$$\begin{array}{cccc}
+ & - & + & - & \cdots \\
- & + & - & + & \cdots \\
+ & - & + & - & \cdots \\
\vdots & \vdots & \vdots & \vdots &
\end{array}$$

Example In a previous Example we have seen that the matrix

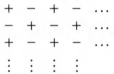

$$A = \begin{bmatrix} 1 & 1 & -1 \\ 2 & 1 & 3 \\ 1 & -5 & 1 \end{bmatrix}$$

is such that $\det A = 28$. By 8.12, therefore, A is invertible. Now the adjugate matrix is

$$
\begin{bmatrix}
\det\begin{bmatrix} 1 & 3 \\ -5 & 1 \end{bmatrix} & -\det\begin{bmatrix} 1 & -1 \\ -5 & 1 \end{bmatrix} & \det\begin{bmatrix} 1 & -1 \\ 1 & 3 \end{bmatrix} \\[2mm]
-\det\begin{bmatrix} 2 & 3 \\ 1 & 1 \end{bmatrix} & \det\begin{bmatrix} 1 & -1 \\ 1 & 1 \end{bmatrix} & -\det\begin{bmatrix} 1 & -1 \\ 2 & 3 \end{bmatrix} \\[2mm]
\det\begin{bmatrix} 2 & 1 \\ 1 & -5 \end{bmatrix} & -\det\begin{bmatrix} 1 & 1 \\ 1 & -5 \end{bmatrix} & \det\begin{bmatrix} 1 & 1 \\ 2 & 1 \end{bmatrix}
\end{bmatrix},
$$

i.e. it is the following matrix (which with practice can be worked out mentally) :

$$
B = \begin{bmatrix}
16 & 4 & 4 \\
1 & 2 & -5 \\
-11 & 6 & -1
\end{bmatrix}.
$$

Then $A^{-1} = \frac{1}{28}B$, which can be verified by direct multiplication.

CHAPTER NINE

Eigenvalues and eigenvectors

Our objective now is to obtain an answer to the question : under what conditions is an $n \times n$ matrix A similar to a diagonal matrix? In so doing, we shall draw together all the notions that have been developed previously. Unless otherwise specified, A will denote an $n \times n$ matrix over $\mathbb{R}$ or $\mathbb{C}$.

Definition By an *eigenvalue* of A we shall mean a scalar λ for which there exists a *non-zero* $n \times 1$ matrix $\mathbf{x}$ such that $A\mathbf{x} = \lambda\mathbf{x}$. Such a (column) matrix $\mathbf{x}$ is called an *eigenvector* associated with λ.

9.1 Theorem λ *is an eigenvalue of A if and only if it is a solution of the equation* $\det(A - \lambda I_n) = 0$.

Proof Observe that $A\mathbf{x} = \lambda\mathbf{x}$ can be written $(A - \lambda I_n)\mathbf{x} = 0$. Then λ is an eigenvalue of A if and only if the system of equations $(A - \lambda I_n)\mathbf{x} = 0$ has a non-zero solution. By 3.17 and 4.2, this is the case if and only if $A - \lambda I_n$ is not invertible, and by 8.12 this is equivalent to $\det(A - \lambda I_n) = 0$. $\diamond$

9.2 Corollary *Similar matrices have the same eigenvalues.*

Proof It suffices to observe that, by 8.10,

$$\det(P^{-1}AP - \lambda I_n) = \det[P^{-1}(A - \lambda I_n)P]$$
$$= \det P^{-1} \cdot \det(A - \lambda I_n) \cdot \det P$$
$$= \det(A - \lambda I_n). \quad \diamond$$

Note that with $A = [a_{ij}]_{n \times n}$ we have

$$\det(A - \lambda I_n) = \det \begin{bmatrix} a_{11} - \lambda & a_{12} & \cdots & a_{1n} \\ a_{21} & a_{22} - \lambda & \cdots & a_{2n} \\ \vdots & \vdots & & \vdots \\ a_{n1} & a_{n2} & \cdots & a_{nn} - \lambda \end{bmatrix}$$

and, by the $\sum_\sigma$-expansion, this is a polynomial of degree n in λ. We call this the *characteristic polynomial* of A. By the *characteristic equation* of A we mean the equation $\det(A - \lambda I_n) = 0$. Thus 9.1 can be expressed by saying that the eigenvalues are the roots of the characteristic equation. Over the field $\mathbb{C}$ of complex numbers this equation has n roots, some of which may be repeated. If $\lambda_1, \ldots, \lambda_k$ are the distinct roots (=eigenvalues) then the characteristic polynomial factorizes in the form

$$(\lambda - \lambda_1)^{r_1}(\lambda - \lambda_2)^{r_2} \cdots (\lambda - \lambda_k)^{r_k}.$$

We call $r_1, \ldots, r_k$ the *algebraic multiplicities* of $\lambda_1, \ldots, \lambda_k$.

Example Consider the matrix

$$A = \begin{bmatrix} 0 & 1 \\ -1 & 0 \end{bmatrix}.$$

We have

$$\det(A - \lambda I_2) = \det \begin{bmatrix} -\lambda & 1 \\ -1 & -\lambda \end{bmatrix} = \lambda^2 + 1.$$

Since $\lambda^2 + 1 = 0$ has no real roots we see that A has no real eigenvalues. However, if we regard A as a matrix over $\mathbb{C}$ then A has two eigenvalues, namely i and $-i$, each being of algebraic multiplicity 1.

Example Consider the matrix

$$A = \begin{bmatrix} -3 & 1 & -1 \\ -7 & 5 & -1 \\ -6 & 6 & -2 \end{bmatrix}.$$

We have, using the obvious row/column operations.

$$\det(A - \lambda I_3) = \det \begin{bmatrix} -3 - \lambda & 1 & -1 \\ -7 & 5 - \lambda & -1 \\ -6 & 6 & -2 - \lambda \end{bmatrix}$$

$$= \det \begin{bmatrix} -2 - \lambda & 1 & -1 \\ -2 - \lambda & 5 - \lambda & -1 \\ 0 & 6 & -2 - \lambda \end{bmatrix}$$

$$= -(2 + \lambda) \det \begin{bmatrix} 1 & 1 & -1 \\ 1 & 5 - \lambda & -1 \\ 0 & 6 & -2 - \lambda \end{bmatrix}$$

$$= -(2 + \lambda) \det \begin{bmatrix} 1 & 1 & -1 \\ 0 & 4 - \lambda & 0 \\ 0 & 6 & -2 - \lambda \end{bmatrix}$$

$$= (2 + \lambda)^2 (4 - \lambda)$$

so the eigenvalues are 4 and -2, the latter being of algebraic multiplicity 2.

If λ is an eigenvalue of A then the set

$$E_\lambda = \{ \mathbf{x} \in \mathrm{Mat}_{n \times 1}(F) ; A\mathbf{x} = \lambda \mathbf{x} \},$$

i.e. the set of eigenvectors corresponding to λ together with the zero column $\mathbf{0}$, is clearly a subspace of $\mathrm{Mat}_{n \times 1}(F)$. This is called the *eigenspace* associated with the eigenvalue λ. The dimension of the eigenspace E_λ is called the *geometric multiplicity* of the eigenvalue λ.

Example Consider the matrix A of the previous Example. The eigenvalues are 4 and -2. To determine the eigenspace E_4, we solve $(A - 4I_3)\mathbf{x} = \mathbf{0}$, i.e.

$$\begin{bmatrix} -7 & 1 & -1 \\ -7 & 1 & -1 \\ -6 & 6 & -6 \end{bmatrix} \begin{bmatrix} x \\ y \\ z \end{bmatrix} = \begin{bmatrix} 0 \\ 0 \\ 0 \end{bmatrix}.$$

The corresponding system of equations reduces to $x = 0, y - z = 0$ and so E_4 is spanned by $\mathbf{x} = [0 \ y \ y]^t$, where $y \neq 0$ since eigenvectors are non-zero by definition. Consequently we see that the eigenspace E_4 is of dimension 1 with basis $\{[0\ 1\ 1]^t\}$.

We proceed in a similar way to determine the eigenspace E_{-2}. We solve $(A + 2I_3)\mathbf{x} = \mathbf{0}$, i.e.

$$\begin{bmatrix} -1 & 1 & -1 \\ -7 & 7 & -1 \\ -6 & 6 & 0 \end{bmatrix} \begin{bmatrix} x \\ y \\ z \end{bmatrix} = \begin{bmatrix} 0 \\ 0 \\ 0 \end{bmatrix}.$$

The corresponding system of equations reduces to $x = y, z = 0$ so E_{-2} is spanned by $\mathbf{x} = [x\ x\ 0]^t$ where $x \neq 0$. Thus E_{-2} is also of dimension 1 with basis $\{[1\ 1\ 0]^t\}$.

The notions of eigenvalue and eigenvector can also be defined for linear mappings. If $f : V \to W$ is linear then a scalar λ is an *eigenvalue* of f if there is a non-zero $x \in V$ such that $f(x) = \lambda x$, such an x being called an *eigenvector* associated with λ. The connection with matrices is as follows. Given an $n \times n$ matrix A, we can consider the linear mapping

$$f_A : \text{Mat}_{n \times 1}(F) \to \text{Mat}_{n \times 1}(F)$$

given by $f_A(\mathbf{x}) = A\mathbf{x}$. It is readily verified that, relative to the standard ordered basis of $\text{Mat}_{n \times 1}(F)$, we have $\text{Mat}\, f_A = A$. Clearly, A and f_A have the same eigenvalues.

Example Consider the vector space $\text{Diff}(\mathbb{R}, \mathbb{R})$ of all differentiable functions $f : \mathbb{R} \to \mathbb{R}$. The differentiation map

$$D : \text{Diff}(\mathbb{R}, \mathbb{R}) \to \text{Map}(\mathbb{R}, \mathbb{R})$$

is linear. An eigenvector of D is a non-zero differentiable function f such that, for some $\lambda \in \mathbb{R}$, $Df = \lambda f$. By the theory of first-order differential equations we see that the eigenvectors of D are therefore the functions $x \mapsto ke^{\lambda x}$ where $k \neq 0$.

Example Consider the linear mapping $f : \mathbb{R}^3 \to \mathbb{R}^3$ given by

$$f(x, y, z) = (y + z, x + z, x + y).$$

Relative to the standard ordered basis the matrix of f is

$$A = \begin{bmatrix} 0 & 1 & 1 \\ 1 & 0 & 1 \\ 1 & 1 & 0 \end{bmatrix}.$$

We now observe that

$$\det(A - \lambda I_3) = \det \begin{bmatrix} -\lambda & 1 & 1 \\ 1 & -\lambda & 1 \\ 1 & 1 & -\lambda \end{bmatrix}$$

$$= \det \begin{bmatrix} -\lambda-1 & 1 & 1 \\ 1+\lambda & -\lambda & 1 \\ 0 & 1 & -\lambda \end{bmatrix}$$

$$= -(1+\lambda)\det \begin{bmatrix} 1 & 1 & 1 \\ -1 & -\lambda & 1 \\ 0 & 1 & -\lambda \end{bmatrix}$$

$$= -(1+\lambda)\det \begin{bmatrix} 1 & 1 & 1 \\ 0 & 1-\lambda & 2 \\ 0 & 1 & -\lambda \end{bmatrix}$$

$$= -(1+\lambda)[\lambda^2 - \lambda - 2]$$

$$= -(1+\lambda)^2(\lambda - 2),$$

so the eigenvalues of A, and hence of f, are 2 and -1, the latter being of algebraic multiplicity 2.

We now establish the following important result.

9.3 Theorem *Eigenvectors that correspond to distinct eigenvalues are linearly independent.*

Proof The proof is by induction. If $f : V \to V$ has only one eigenvalue and if x is a corresponding eigenvector then since $x \neq 0$ we know that $\{x\}$ is linearly independent. For the inductive step, suppose that every set of n eigenvectors that correspond to n distinct eigenvalues is linearly independent, and let $x_1, \ldots, x_{n+1}$ be eigenvectors that correspond to distinct eigenvalues $\lambda_1, \ldots, \lambda_{n+1}$. If we have

$$(1) \qquad a_1 x_1 + \cdots + a_n x_n + a_{n+1} x_{n+1} = 0$$

then, applying f to each side and using the fact that $f(x_i) = \lambda_i x_i$, we obtain

$$(2) \qquad a_1 \lambda_1 x_1 + \cdots + a_n \lambda_n x_n + a_{n+1} \lambda_{n+1} x_{n+1} = 0.$$

Now take $(2) - \lambda_{n+1}(1)$ to get

$$a_1(\lambda_1 - \lambda_{n+1})x_1 + \cdots + a_n(\lambda_n - \lambda_{n+1})x_n = 0.$$

By the induction hypothesis and the fact that $\lambda_1, \ldots, \lambda_{n+1}$ are distinct, we deduce that $a_1 = \cdots = a_n = 0$. It now follows by (1) that $a_{n+1}x_{n+1} = 0$ whence, since $x_{n+1} \neq 0$, we also have $a_{n+1} = 0$. Hence $x_1, \ldots, x_{n+1}$ are linearly independent and the result follows. $\diamond$

Consider now a linear mapping $f : V \to V$ where V is of dimension n. It is clear that f is *diagonalizable*, i.e. can be represented by a diagonal matrix

$$\begin{bmatrix} \lambda_1 & & & \\ & \lambda_2 & & \\ & & \ddots & \\ & & & \lambda_n \end{bmatrix},$$

if and only if there is an ordered basis $(v_i)_n$ of V such that

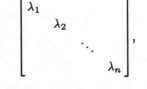

$$\begin{aligned} f(v_1) &= \lambda_1 v_1 \\ f(v_2) &= \quad\; \lambda_2 v_2 \\ &\;\; \vdots \qquad\qquad \ddots \\ f(v_n) &= \qquad\qquad\qquad \lambda_n v_n \end{aligned}$$

We can therefore state :

9.4 Theorem *A linear mapping $f : V \to V$ can be represented by a diagonal matrix D if and only if V has a basis consisting of eigenvectors of f. In this case the diagonal entries of D are the eigenvalues of f.* $\diamond$

Equivalently, as a result on matrices :

9.4' Theorem *An $n \times n$ matrix A is similar to a diagonal matrix D if and only if A has n linearly independent eigenvectors. In this case the diagonal entries of D are the eigenvalues of A.* $\diamond$

We say that an $n \times n$ matrix A is *diagonalizable* if it is similar to a diagonal matrix D, i.e. if there is an invertible matrix P

such that $P^{-1}AP = D$. We shall now consider the problem of finding such a matrix P. First we observe that the equation $P^{-1}AP = D$ can be written $AP = PD$. Let the columns of P be $\mathbf{p}_1, \ldots, \mathbf{p}_n$ and let

$$D = \begin{bmatrix} \lambda_1 & & & \\ & \lambda_2 & & \\ & & \ddots & \\ & & & \lambda_n \end{bmatrix}$$

where $\lambda_1, \ldots, \lambda_n$ are the eigenvalues of A. Comparing the i-th columns of each side of the equation $AP = PD$, we obtain

$$(i = 1, \ldots, n) \qquad A\mathbf{p}_i = \lambda_i \mathbf{p}_i.$$

In other words, *the i-th column of P is an eigenvector of A corresponding to the eigenvalue λ_i*.

Example As observed in the second Example of this Chapter, the matrix

$$A = \begin{bmatrix} -3 & 1 & -1 \\ -7 & 5 & -1 \\ -6 & 6 & -2 \end{bmatrix}$$

has only two distinct eigenvalues, namely 4 and -2, the latter being of algebraic multiplicity 2. Also, as seen in the third Example, each of these eigenvalues is of geometric multiplicity 1 (i.e. in each case the dimension of the associated eigenspace is 1). Consequently, A cannot have three linearly independent eigenvectors and so, by 9.4', A is not diagonalizable.

Example Consider the matrix

$$B = \begin{bmatrix} 1 & -3 & 3 \\ 3 & -5 & 3 \\ 6 & -6 & 4 \end{bmatrix}.$$

The reader can readily verify that

$$\det(B - \lambda I_3) = (4 - \lambda)(\lambda + 2)^2,$$

so the eigenvalues are also 4 and -2, the latter being of algebraic multiplicity 2.

To determine the eigenspace E_{-2} we solve $(B + 2I_3)\mathbf{x} = 0$, i.e.

$$\begin{bmatrix} 3 & -3 & 3 \\ 3 & -3 & 3 \\ 6 & -6 & 6 \end{bmatrix} \begin{bmatrix} x \\ y \\ z \end{bmatrix} = \begin{bmatrix} 0 \\ 0 \\ 0 \end{bmatrix}.$$

The corresponding system of equations reduces to $x - y + z = 0$, so the coefficient matrix is of rank 1 and so the dimension of the solution space is $3 - 1 = 2$. Thus the eigenvalue -2 is of geometric multiplicity 2. Two linearly independent eigenvectors in E_{-2} will then form a basis for E_{-2}. For these we can choose, for example,

$$\begin{bmatrix} 1 \\ 1 \\ 0 \end{bmatrix}, \quad \begin{bmatrix} 1 \\ 0 \\ -1 \end{bmatrix}.$$

To determine the eigenspace E_4 we solve $(B - 4I_3)\mathbf{x} = 0$, i.e.

$$\begin{bmatrix} -3 & -3 & 3 \\ 3 & -9 & 3 \\ 6 & -6 & 0 \end{bmatrix} \begin{bmatrix} x \\ y \\ z \end{bmatrix} = \begin{bmatrix} 0 \\ 0 \\ 0 \end{bmatrix}.$$

The corresponding system of equations reduces to

$$x + y - z = 0$$
$$2y - z = 0$$

so the rank of the coefficient matrix is 2, and the solution space is of dimension $3 - 2 = 1$. Any single non-zero vector in E_4 will then constitute a basis for E_4. We can choose, for example,

$$\begin{bmatrix} 1 \\ 1 \\ 2 \end{bmatrix}.$$

Clearly, the above three eigenvectors are linearly independent. Hence, by 9.4', B is diagonalizable. Pasting together the above eigenvectors we obtain the matrix

$$P = \begin{bmatrix} 1 & 1 & 1 \\ 1 & 0 & 1 \\ 0 & -1 & 2 \end{bmatrix},$$

which is such that

$$P^{-1}BP = \begin{bmatrix} -2 & 0 & 0 \\ 0 & -2 & 0 \\ 0 & 0 & 4 \end{bmatrix}.$$

Let us now return to the problems of equilibrium-seeking systems and difference equations, as outlined in Chapter Two. In each of these the matrix considered is of size 2×2, so we first prove a useful result that will help cut a few corners.

9.5 Theorem *If the 2×2 matrix*

$$A = \begin{bmatrix} a & b \\ c & d \end{bmatrix}$$

has distinct eigenvalues λ_1, λ_2 then it is diagonalizable. An invertible matrix P such that

$$P^{-1}AP = \begin{bmatrix} \lambda_1 & 0 \\ 0 & \lambda_2 \end{bmatrix}$$

is the matrix

$$P = \begin{bmatrix} b & b \\ \lambda_1 - a & \lambda_2 - a \end{bmatrix}.$$

Proof The first statement is immediate from 9.3 and 9.4′. As for the second statement, we observe that

$$\det \begin{bmatrix} a - \lambda & b \\ c & d - \lambda \end{bmatrix} = \lambda^2 - (a + d)\lambda + ad - bc$$

and so the eigenvalues of A are

$$\lambda_1 = \tfrac{1}{2}[(a + d) + \sqrt{(a - d)^2 + 4bc}],$$
$$\lambda_2 = \tfrac{1}{2}[(a + d) - \sqrt{(a - d)^2 + 4bc}].$$

Consider the column matrix

$$\mathbf{x}_1 = \begin{bmatrix} b \\ \lambda_1 - a \end{bmatrix}.$$

We have $\quad A\,x_1 = \lambda_1 x_1$

$$\begin{bmatrix} a & b \\ c & d \end{bmatrix} \begin{bmatrix} b \\ \lambda_1 - a \end{bmatrix} = \begin{bmatrix} b\lambda_1 \\ cb + d(\lambda_1 - a) \end{bmatrix} = \lambda_1 \begin{bmatrix} b \\ \lambda_1 - a \end{bmatrix},$$

the final equality resulting from the fact that

$$\lambda_1(\lambda_1 - a) - cb - d(\lambda_1 - a) = \lambda_1^2 - (a + d)\lambda_1 + ad - bc$$

$$\lambda_1(\lambda_1 - a) \qquad = 0. \quad cb + d(\lambda_1 - a)$$

Thus $\mathbf{x}_1$ is an eigenvector associated with λ_1. Similarly, we can show that

$$\mathbf{x}_2 = \begin{bmatrix} b \\ \lambda_2 - a \end{bmatrix} \qquad p = (x_1 | x_2)$$

is an eigenvector associated with λ_2. Pasting these eigenvectors together, we obtain the required matrix P. $\diamond$

Example Consider the equilibrium-seeking system described in Chapter Two. The matrix in question is

$$A = \begin{bmatrix} \frac{1}{4} & \frac{1}{20} \\ \frac{3}{4} & \frac{19}{20} \end{bmatrix}.$$

The eigenvalues of A are the roots of

$$\left(\tfrac{1}{4} - \lambda\right)\left(\tfrac{19}{20} - \lambda\right) - \tfrac{3}{80} = 0.$$

The reader will easily check that this reduces to

$$(5\lambda - 1)(\lambda - 1) = 0$$

so that the eigenvalues are $\frac{1}{5}$ and 1. It follows by 9.5 that A is diagonalizable, that an eigenvector associated with $\lambda_1 = \frac{1}{5}$ is

$$\begin{bmatrix} \frac{1}{20} \\ \frac{1}{5} - \frac{1}{4} \end{bmatrix} = \begin{bmatrix} \frac{1}{20} \\ -\frac{1}{20} \end{bmatrix},$$

$$\begin{bmatrix} b \\ \lambda_1 - a \end{bmatrix}$$

and that an eigenvector associated with $\lambda_2 = 1$ is

$$\begin{bmatrix} \frac{1}{20} \\ 1 - \frac{1}{4} \end{bmatrix} = \begin{bmatrix} \frac{1}{20} \\ \frac{3}{4} \end{bmatrix}.$$

We can therefore assert that the matrix

$$P = \begin{bmatrix} 1 & 1 \\ -1 & 15 \end{bmatrix}$$

is invertible and

$$P^{-1}AP = \begin{bmatrix} \frac{1}{5} & 0 \\ 0 & 1 \end{bmatrix}.$$

Since, as is readily seen,

$$P^{-1} = \frac{1}{16} \begin{bmatrix} 15 & -1 \\ 1 & 1 \end{bmatrix},$$

we can compute

$$A^n = \frac{1}{16} \begin{bmatrix} 1 & 1 \\ -1 & 15 \end{bmatrix} \begin{bmatrix} \frac{1}{5^n} & 0 \\ 0 & 1 \end{bmatrix} \begin{bmatrix} 15 & -1 \\ 1 & 1 \end{bmatrix}$$

$$= \frac{1}{16} \begin{bmatrix} 1 & 1 \\ -1 & 15 \end{bmatrix} \begin{bmatrix} \frac{15}{5^n} & -\frac{1}{5^n} \\ 1 & 1 \end{bmatrix}$$

$$= \frac{1}{16} \begin{bmatrix} 1 + \frac{15}{5^n} & 1 - \frac{1}{5^n} \\ 15(1 - \frac{1}{5^n}) & 15 + \frac{1}{5^n} \end{bmatrix}.$$

Example Consider the *Fibonacci sequence* $(a_i)_{i \geq 1}$ defined recursively by $a_0 = 0, a_1 = 1$ and

$$(\forall n \geq 0) \qquad a_{n+2} = a_{n+1} + a_n.$$

We can write this as a system of difference equations in the following way :

$$a_{n+2} = a_{n+1} + b_{n+1}$$
$$b_{n+2} = a_{n+1}.$$

This we can represent in matrix form as $\mathbf{X}_{n+2} = A\mathbf{X}_{n+1}$ where

$$A = \begin{bmatrix} 1 & 1 \\ 1 & 0 \end{bmatrix}.$$

The eigenvalues of A are the solutions of $\lambda^2 - \lambda - 1 = 0$, i.e. they are

$$\lambda_1 = \tfrac{1}{2}(1 + \sqrt{5}), \qquad \lambda_2 = \tfrac{1}{2}(1 - \sqrt{5}).$$

By 9.5, A is diagonalizable and corresponding eigenvectors are

$$\begin{bmatrix} 1 \\ \lambda_1 - 1 \end{bmatrix} = \begin{bmatrix} 1 \\ -\lambda_2 \end{bmatrix} \quad \text{and} \quad \begin{bmatrix} 1 \\ \lambda_2 - 1 \end{bmatrix} = \begin{bmatrix} 1 \\ -\lambda_1 \end{bmatrix}.$$

Then the matrix

$$P = \begin{bmatrix} 1 & 1 \\ -\lambda_2 & -\lambda_1 \end{bmatrix}$$

is invertible and such that

$$P^{-1}AP = \begin{bmatrix} \lambda_1 & 0 \\ 0 & \lambda_2 \end{bmatrix}.$$

Now clearly

$$P^{-1} = \tfrac{1}{\lambda_2 - \lambda_1} \begin{bmatrix} -\lambda_1 & -1 \\ \lambda_2 & 1 \end{bmatrix}$$

and so, using the fact that $\lambda_1 \lambda_2 = -1$, we can compute

$$
\begin{aligned}
A^n &= \tfrac{1}{\lambda_2 - \lambda_1} \begin{bmatrix} 1 & 1 \\ -\lambda_2 & -\lambda_1 \end{bmatrix} \begin{bmatrix} \lambda_1^n & 0 \\ 0 & \lambda_2^n \end{bmatrix} \begin{bmatrix} -\lambda_1 & -1 \\ \lambda_2 & 1 \end{bmatrix} \\
&= \tfrac{1}{\lambda_2 - \lambda_1} \begin{bmatrix} 1 & 1 \\ -\lambda_2 & -\lambda_1 \end{bmatrix} \begin{bmatrix} -\lambda_1^{n+1} & -\lambda_1^n \\ \lambda_2^{n+1} & \lambda_2^n \end{bmatrix} \\
&= \tfrac{1}{\lambda_2 - \lambda_1} \begin{bmatrix} \lambda_2^{n+1} - \lambda_1^{n+1} & \lambda_2^n - \lambda_1^n \\ \lambda_2^n - \lambda_1^n & \lambda_2^{n-1} - \lambda_1^{n-1} \end{bmatrix}.
\end{aligned}
$$

Since it is given that $b_1 = a_0 = 0$ and $a_1 = 1$, we can now assert that

$$\begin{bmatrix} a_{n+1} \\ b_{n+1} \end{bmatrix} = A^n \mathbf{X}_1 = A^n \begin{bmatrix} 1 \\ 0 \end{bmatrix}$$

$$= \frac{1}{\lambda_2 - \lambda_1} \begin{bmatrix} \lambda_2^{n+1} - \lambda_1^{n+1} \\ \lambda_2^n - \lambda_1^n \end{bmatrix}$$

and hence we see that

$$a_n = \frac{1}{\lambda_2 - \lambda_1}(\lambda_2^n - \lambda_1^n)$$
$$= \frac{1}{\sqrt{5}}[\tfrac{1}{2}(1 + \sqrt{5})]^n - \frac{1}{\sqrt{5}}[\tfrac{1}{2}(1 - \sqrt{5})]^n.$$

Example Consider the sequence of fractions

$$2, \quad 2 + \tfrac{1}{2}, \quad 2 + \frac{1}{2 + \tfrac{1}{2}}, \quad 2 + \cfrac{1}{2 + \cfrac{1}{2 + \tfrac{1}{2}}}, \quad \ldots .$$

This is a particular example of what is called a *continued fraction*. If we denote the n-th term in this sequence by $\dfrac{a_n}{b_n}$ then we have

$$\frac{a_{n+1}}{b_{n+1}} = 2 + \frac{1}{\dfrac{a_n}{b_n}} = \frac{2a_n + b_n}{a_n}$$

so we can consider the difference equations

$$a_{n+1} = 2a_n + b_n$$
$$b_{n+1} = a_n.$$

The matrix of the system is

$$A = \begin{bmatrix} 2 & 1 \\ 1 & 0 \end{bmatrix},$$

and we can write the system as $\mathbf{X}_{n+1} = A\mathbf{X}_n$. Now $a_1 = 2$ and $b_1 = 1$ so we can compute $\mathbf{X}_{n+1}$ from

$$\mathbf{X}_{n+1} = A^n \begin{bmatrix} 2 \\ 1 \end{bmatrix}.$$

The eigenvalues of A are the solutions of $\lambda^2 - 2\lambda - 1 = 0$, i.e. they are

$$\lambda_1 = 1 + \sqrt{2}, \qquad \lambda_2 = 1 - \sqrt{2}.$$

By 9.5, the matrix

$$P = \begin{bmatrix} 1 & 1 \\ -1 + \sqrt{2} & -1 - \sqrt{2} \end{bmatrix} = \begin{bmatrix} 1 & 1 \\ -\lambda_2 & -\lambda_1 \end{bmatrix}$$

is invertible and such that

$$P^{-1}AP = \begin{bmatrix} 1 + \sqrt{2} & 0 \\ 0 & 1 - \sqrt{2} \end{bmatrix}.$$

Now it is readily seen that

$$P^{-1} = \tfrac{1}{2\sqrt{2}} \begin{bmatrix} 1 + \sqrt{2} & 1 \\ -1 + \sqrt{2} & -1 \end{bmatrix} = \tfrac{1}{2\sqrt{2}} \begin{bmatrix} \lambda_1 & 1 \\ -\lambda_2 & -1 \end{bmatrix}.$$

Consequently,

$$\begin{aligned}
A^n &= \tfrac{1}{2\sqrt{2}} \begin{bmatrix} 1 & 1 \\ -\lambda_2 & -\lambda_1 \end{bmatrix} \begin{bmatrix} \lambda_1^n & 0 \\ 0 & \lambda_2^n \end{bmatrix} \begin{bmatrix} \lambda_1 & 1 \\ -\lambda_2 & -1 \end{bmatrix} \\
&= \tfrac{1}{2\sqrt{2}} \begin{bmatrix} 1 & 1 \\ -\lambda_2 & -\lambda_1 \end{bmatrix} \begin{bmatrix} \lambda_1^{n+1} & \lambda_1^n \\ -\lambda_2^{n+1} & -\lambda_2^n \end{bmatrix} \\
&= \tfrac{1}{2\sqrt{2}} \begin{bmatrix} \lambda_1^{n+1} - \lambda_2^{n+1} & \lambda_1^n - \lambda_2^n \\ \lambda_1^n - \lambda_2^n & \lambda_1^{n-1} - \lambda_2^{n-1} \end{bmatrix}
\end{aligned}$$

and so we deduce from

$$\begin{bmatrix} a_{n+1} \\ b_{n+1} \end{bmatrix} = A^n \begin{bmatrix} 2 \\ 1 \end{bmatrix}$$

that the general term $\dfrac{a_{n+1}}{b_{n+1}}$ is given by

$$\frac{2[(1 + \sqrt{2})^{n+1} - (1 - \sqrt{2})^{n+1}] + (1 + \sqrt{2})^n - (1 - \sqrt{2})^n}{2[(1 + \sqrt{2})^n - (1 - \sqrt{2})^n] + (1 + \sqrt{2})^{n-1} - (1 - \sqrt{2})^{n-1}}.$$

Example If q_1 is a positive rational define

$$q_2 = \frac{2+q_1}{1+q_1}.$$

Then it is easy to show that $|2-q_2^2| < |2-q_1^2|$. In other words, if q_1 is an approximation to $\sqrt{2}$ then q_2 is a better approximation. Starting with $q_1 = 1$ and applying this observation repeatedly, we obtain the sequence

$$1, \quad \frac{3}{2}, \quad \frac{7}{5}, \quad \frac{17}{12}, \quad \frac{41}{29}, \quad \frac{99}{70}, \quad \cdots$$

We can use the techniques described above to determine the general term in this sequence and show that it does indeed converge to $\sqrt{2}$. Denoting the n-th term by $\dfrac{a_n}{b_n}$ we have

$$\frac{a_{n+1}}{b_{n+1}} = \frac{2+\dfrac{a_n}{b_n}}{1+\dfrac{a_n}{b_n}} = \frac{2b_n + a_n}{b_n + a_n}$$

and so the sequence is described by the system of difference equations

$$a_{n+1} = a_n + 2b_n$$
$$b_{n+1} = a_n + b_n.$$

The matrix of the system is

$$A = \begin{bmatrix} 1 & 2 \\ 1 & 1 \end{bmatrix}$$

and its characteristic equation is $\lambda^2 - 2\lambda - 1 = 0$, so that the eigenvalues are

$$\lambda_1 = 1 + \sqrt{2} \quad \text{and} \quad \lambda_2 = 1 - \sqrt{2}.$$

By 9.5 the matrix

$$P = \begin{bmatrix} 2 & 2 \\ \sqrt{2} & -\sqrt{2} \end{bmatrix}$$

is invertible and such that

$$P^{-1}AP = \begin{bmatrix} 1+\sqrt{2} & 0 \\ 0 & 1-\sqrt{2} \end{bmatrix}.$$

Now it is readily seen that

$$P^{-1} = \frac{1}{4}\begin{bmatrix} 1 & \sqrt{2} \\ 1 & -\sqrt{2} \end{bmatrix}.$$

Consequently

$$A^n = \frac{1}{4}\begin{bmatrix} 2 & 2 \\ \sqrt{2} & -\sqrt{2} \end{bmatrix}\begin{bmatrix} \lambda_1^n & 0 \\ 0 & \lambda_2^n \end{bmatrix}\begin{bmatrix} 1 & \sqrt{2} \\ 1 & -\sqrt{2} \end{bmatrix}$$

$$= \frac{1}{4}\begin{bmatrix} 2 & 2 \\ \sqrt{2} & -\sqrt{2} \end{bmatrix}\begin{bmatrix} \lambda_1^n & \sqrt{2}\lambda_1^n \\ \lambda_2^n & -\sqrt{2}\lambda_2^n \end{bmatrix}$$

$$= \frac{1}{4}\begin{bmatrix} 2\lambda_1^n + 2\lambda_2^n & 2\sqrt{2}\lambda_1^n - 2\sqrt{2}\lambda_2^n \\ \sqrt{2}\lambda_1^n - \sqrt{2}\lambda_2^n & 2\lambda_1^n + 2\lambda_2^n \end{bmatrix}$$

and so we deduce from

$$\begin{bmatrix} a_{n+1} \\ b_{n+1} \end{bmatrix} = A^n\begin{bmatrix} 1 \\ 1 \end{bmatrix}$$

that

$$\frac{a_{n+1}}{b_{n+1}} = \frac{2(1+\sqrt{2})^{n+1} + 2(1-\sqrt{2})^{n+1}}{\sqrt{2}(1+\sqrt{2})^{n+1} - \sqrt{2}(1-\sqrt{2})^{n+1}}$$

$$= \sqrt{2} \cdot \frac{1 + \left(\frac{1-\sqrt{2}}{1+\sqrt{2}}\right)^{n+1}}{1 - \left(\frac{1-\sqrt{2}}{1+\sqrt{2}}\right)^{n+1}},$$

from which we see that

$$\lim_{n \to \infty} \frac{a_n}{b_n} = \sqrt{2}.$$

It is of course possible for problems such as the above to involve a 2×2 matrix A whose eigenvalues are not distinct. In this case A is not diagonalizable; for if λ is the only eigenvalue then the system of equations $(A - \lambda I_2)\mathbf{x} = \mathbf{0}$ reduces to a single equation and the dimension of the solution space is $2 - 1 = 1$, so there cannot exist two linearly independent eigenvectors. To find high powers of A in this case, we have to proceed in a different manner. If

$$A = \begin{bmatrix} a & b \\ c & d \end{bmatrix}$$

then the characteristic polynomial of A is

$$f(X) = X^2 - (a + d)X + ad - bc.$$

Observe now that

$$A^2 = \begin{bmatrix} a^2 + bc & b(a + d) \\ c(a + d) & bc + d^2 \end{bmatrix}$$

$$= (a + d)\begin{bmatrix} a & b \\ c & d \end{bmatrix} - (ad - bc)\begin{bmatrix} 1 & 0 \\ 0 & 1 \end{bmatrix}$$

$$= (a + d)A - (ad - bc)I_2$$

and so we see that $f(A) = 0$. For $n \geq 2$ consider the euclidean division of X^n by $f(X)$; since f is of degree 2, we have

$$(\star) \qquad X^n = f(X)q(X) + \alpha_1 X + \alpha_2.$$

Substituting A for X in this polynomial identity we obtain, by the above observation,

$$A^n = \alpha_1 A + \alpha_2 I_2.$$

We can determine α_1 and α_2 as follows. If we differentiate $(\star)$ and substitute λ (the single eigenvalue of A) for X then, since $f(\lambda) = 0$, we obtain

$$n\lambda^{n-1} = \alpha_1.$$

Also, substituting λ for X in $(\star)$ and again using $f(\lambda) = 0$, we obtain

$$\lambda^n = \alpha_1 \lambda + \alpha_2 = n\lambda^n + \alpha_2$$

and so

$$\alpha_2 = (1 - n)\lambda^n.$$

It now follows that

$$A^n = n\lambda^{n-1}A + (1-n)\lambda^n I_2.$$

Example Consider the $n \times n$ matrix

$$A_n = \begin{bmatrix} 2 & 1 & 0 & 0 & \cdots & 0 & 0 \\ 1 & 2 & 1 & 0 & \cdots & 0 & 0 \\ 0 & 1 & 2 & 1 & \cdots & 0 & 0 \\ \vdots & \vdots & \vdots & \vdots & & \vdots & \vdots \\ 0 & 0 & 0 & 0 & \cdots & 2 & 1 \\ 0 & 0 & 0 & 0 & \cdots & 1 & 2 \end{bmatrix}.$$

Writing $a_n = \det A_n$ we have, using a Laplace expansion along the first row,

$$a_n = 2a_{n-1} - \det \begin{bmatrix} 1 & 1 & 0 & 0 & \cdots & 0 \\ 0 & 2 & 1 & 0 & \cdots & 0 \\ 0 & 1 & 2 & 1 & \cdots & 0 \\ \vdots & \vdots & \vdots & \vdots & & \vdots \\ 0 & 0 & 0 & 0 & \cdots & 2 \end{bmatrix}$$

$$= 2a_{n-1} - a_{n-2}.$$

Writing this recurrence relation in the usual way as a system of difference equations

$$a_n = 2a_{n-1} - b_{n-1}$$
$$b_n = a_{n-1}$$

we consider the system $\mathbf{X}_n = A\mathbf{X}_{n-1}$ where

$$A = \begin{bmatrix} 2 & -1 \\ 1 & 0 \end{bmatrix}.$$

Now

$$\det(A - \lambda I_2) = \lambda(\lambda - 2) + 1 = (\lambda - 1)^2,$$

and so A has the single eigenvalue 1 of algebraic multiplicity 2. We can compute A^n as in the above :

$$A^n = nA + (1-n)I_2$$
$$= \begin{bmatrix} n+1 & -n \\ n & 1-n \end{bmatrix}.$$

Consequently we have

$$\begin{bmatrix} a_n \\ b_n \end{bmatrix} = A^{n-2} \begin{bmatrix} a_2 \\ b_2 \end{bmatrix} = A^{n-2} \begin{bmatrix} a_2 \\ a_1 \end{bmatrix}$$
$$= \begin{bmatrix} n-1 & -n+2 \\ n-2 & 3-n \end{bmatrix} \begin{bmatrix} 3 \\ 2 \end{bmatrix}$$
$$= \begin{bmatrix} n+1 \\ n \end{bmatrix}$$

and hence we see that

$$\det A_n = a_n = n+1.$$

Index